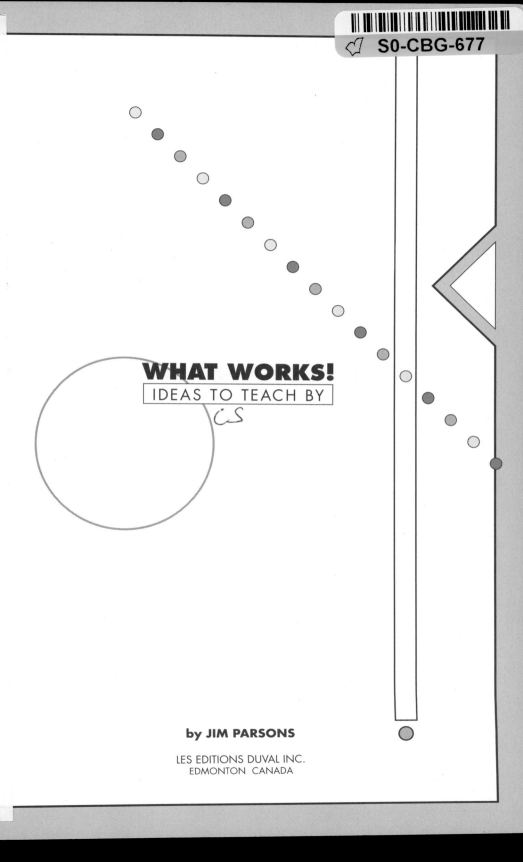

# WHAT WORKS!

## IDEAS TO TEACH BY

**by JIM PARSONS**

LES EDITIONS DUVAL INC.
EDMONTON CANADA

© 1992 Les Editions Duval Inc.

Les Editions Duval Inc.
#111A, The Lemarchand Mansion
11523 - 100 Ave.,
Edmonton, Alberta
CANADA T5K 0J8
(403) 482-4845

Design and Production by Pièce de Résistance Ltée.,
Printed by Quality Color Press Ltd.


First printing: December 1992

**Canadian Cataloguing in Publication Data**

Parsons, Jim, 1948–
    What Works

    Includes index.          *Toc*
    ISBN 1-895850-06-1

    1.  Teaching.  I. Title
LB1037.P37  1992        371.1'02    C93-091114-8

## DEDICATION

I would like to dedicate this work to Jim Parsons, my father.
He taught me that "the world didn't owe me a living."
He also taught me that a person can live simply, honestly,
and can give good return on an investment.

# TABLE OF CONTENTS

## Part I: Being a Teacher

# Part II: Ideas for Teaching

# PART I
## Being a Teacher

# HOW TO SET YOUR TEACHING GOALS

## WHY SET GOALS?

Setting teaching goals may seem like a strange subject in a book written to provide teaching ideas, but I think this may be the most important teaching idea in the book. I'll try to answer why, before I answer how.

Some people may have picked up this book looking for something to add to their bag of teaching tricks. In one sense, I hope they are not disappointed. But teaching is more than a bag of tricks. Before any good teaching can take place, it is important to know where you are coming from and where you want to go as a teacher. Ultimately, teaching is more than just having a lesson plan that is well-structured and keeps the students busy and on task.

There is, and should be, a central core to your teaching—a core built upon your beliefs about what teaching is, how it should be done, and why you are doing it. This core includes the things that you stand for. These are things that don't change, regardless of the content you are teaching. I am talking about the need to build, for yourself, a moral and ethical base that governs your work.

Teaching is more than giving students content, at least in the traditional sense of content. Many people have filled their heads with vast amounts of information, but they will never be good teachers. They don't know what they are doing because they don't know why they are doing what they are doing.

I once saw an article titled "100 Things to Do in the Classroom." It was just as it promised, and without any explanation, filled with 100 things to do. The whole article missed the point. Teaching is a reasoned set of activities working toward a particular set of considered goals. Teaching is not a bag of tricks used to entertain or keep students busy.

## HOW TO SET GOALS

How do you set your goals? Let me offer three suggestions from my own experience as a teacher: think, remember, and read. Think about what's important to you. Remember what made a difference, either bad or good, in your own life—particularly your life as a student. And, read and consider what other people say. Read both the lines and between the lines. Work toward a small set of goals, generally stated, so that you can justify what you do in your own head and in front of those who may ask you about them. Here's a note. Like in the movie *Field of Dreams*, if you build these goals, people will ask!

If you are a young teacher just starting out, these goals will help you both center your work and spur you on when you need to be spurred on. When times get tough, and in teaching they will sometimes get very tough, cling to your goals. This may sound very idealistic, but you might want to read a biography about Gandhi, Mother Teresa, or another favorite hero and be inspired by how the notion of truth encouraged their actions. You probably will not be called to save a subcontinent, but there are times when you will feel you have been. Don't let anyone kid you: teaching is, in its own way, heroic.

Enough introduction, here's my own set of five teaching principles. I use these to organize and ground my own teaching, regardless of what it is and where it takes place. I list them early in this book to make the pedagogy and the methodologies of the rest of the book more apparent.

## My Grounds for Teaching: What Do I Believe?

I believe that...

### Knowledge is important in social studies.

With deference to my vegetarian friends, I believe teaching should have "meat." No teaching is good unless it is rich in content. I believe it helps to know things. For me, the statement isn't just hype. My teaching experience and reading of research suggests that as students gain knowledge they also become more confident, more powerful, and more courageous. In short, they become better learners. These are also the very characteristics I believe active, democratic citizens should possess.

As you read the rest of this text, I hope you will see ways you might work to help your students become more knowledgeable. For example, the puzzles you will find in this book may seem only to be games; and I admit I include gaming techniques because students enjoy them. But these activities also serve other purposes. They force students to reread content, refocussing on important facts and concepts. It's that re-reading, that re-focusing, that helps students learn and remember the content.

I believe in giving comprehensive final exams. I want my students to both know and to know that they know. But I also include activities that help students learn the vocabulary, the facts, and the concepts prior to taking this final test. I will never apologize that my activities and tests contain both a depth and breadth of content. My teaching task is not to make things easy, but to teach content to students and to help them become more powerful critical thinkers.

*The task of teaching is to teach.*

I believe that the job of every teacher is to help every student in every class learn all the knowledge, all the attitudes, and all the skills that are included in every curriculum topic. I know that theory and practice differ; still, the goal of teaching all the knowledge to all the students will remain my standard for judging my accomplishment. In every way I can, I try to help my students learn.

With this goal in mind, I create both textbooks and teachers' guides. When I create textbooks and guides, I highlight new and important vocabulary. For example, if the publisher will allow me, I define new and important words at the bottom of the page where they are first used. I consider research on redundancy. Redundancy in this case is the necessary repetition of key material. I choose photographs to mirror narrative content. I write photo captions to carefully repeat important ideas within the narrative as well. I use case studies as specific examples of general ideas. And throughout the teachers' guides I write, I include activities that are both fun and redundant. I do these things to help students review and learn the material I have included in the text.

Every one of you will be both a teacher and a teacher within a jurisdiction. I am an Alberta teacher. This means that I must take care to know and understand my legal responsibility to help teachers ensure that the Alberta curriculum's lists of important concepts, facts, attitudes, and skills have been taught in both my texts and teachers' guides.

*Review is a key teaching technique for all areas and at all levels.*

I know that if teachers really want their students to learn the material in the textbook, going over material once is never enough. Most students forget. I remember that many successful students, if they wanted to do well on exams, wrote sample exam questions on note cards, going over and over these cards as their way to review.

I believe I can help teachers help their students do the same things. When I write a teachers' guide, I construct many little reviews for students. As a junior high school teacher, I developed and used an idea I called creative redundancy. This concept was based on the following questions: How many ways can I help students review the same material using new and different methods? How can I repeat the important content, as prescribed by the curriculum, without being repetitive and boring?

In this book of ideas, you will find ideas to help students engage in creative redundancy—games, flash cards, puzzles, quizzes, writings, debates, reviews, readings, case studies, surveys, and so on. I want students to learn curriculum content and to become more confident that they can and will do well on their evaluations. My theory is quite simple: if students have successful school experiences, they are likely to carry their success throughout life. My first priority as a teacher is political. I want to help my students become powerful, contributing citizens. Teaching them the content of the curriculum is one tool I have to help my students grow toward my political goal.

### Follow the Golden Rule of Teaching

I call this my "Golden Rule of Teaching." If there's a choice between having fun and not having fun, have fun. If there's a choice between being active and not being active, be active. It didn't take me long as a first-year teacher to learn that junior high students were interested in having fun and being active! I also learned that I couldn't fight their desire for fun and activity; but I did learn to use these natural desires to the class's advantage. I learned, whenever possible, to find ways to incorporate the students' natural inclinations for movement, for socializing, and for action into my teaching in a positive way. The only other choice I had was to fight them every step of the way and create a negative experience for everyone in the classroom, including myself. Here's another hint: if you fight your students, you can't win.

I believe that teaching can and should be enjoyable. This doesn't mean that I think a teacher should be a wimp, neither teaching anything nor living without discipline or structure. Quite the contrary. It means that teachers can work to make learning more fun and more active. Puzzles, contests, drills, games, projects, tests (yes, even tests!) have, for me, been successful and enjoyable teaching experiences. I encourage you to have as much active fun as you can.

### Students have many skills to learn.

Skills and content work together as students learn. When I write a teachers' guide, it always includes suggestions for helping students take notes, work on maps and learn geography, use charts and graphs, learn how to organize thoughts, advance skills in writing and proofreading, and work on reading skills. I believe that all teachers are reading teachers. I try to make sure that all my work introduces ways to help students improve their reading and writing skills in natural, rather than contrived, ways.

I stress two skills specifically in my work: reading and vocabulary development. The body of research knowledge shows a high correlation between self-esteem and the ability to read. For this reason alone, I believe it is good to help students improve their reading. In this book of ideas, I have tried to design a number of specific pedagogical techniques that can be used to help students learn to read more fluently. I hope they will help you as a teacher.

### In Conclusion

These may not be your principles, but they are good ones and I would recommend them. I hope that these notes will help you make important choices about how you will read the rest of this text, and how you might make your own teaching more fruitful. The point is this: you must make your own list of principles and let that list ground your actions. Do it now, even though you realize that these ideas may change, grow, and develop. I wish you the best in this important enterprise.

## The Rest of the Book

Ideas are like money in the bank. You can use them, or let them lie. I encourage you to use the ideas in this book, but only if they prove helpful. Otherwise, please do your own thing. In creating this book of ideas, I have tried to respond to suggestions from teachers who have used my ideas in the past. I have also tried to listen carefully when teachers have talked about what they need. Some of the ideas in this book address specific needs they have noted.

I owe many of these ideas to the vision of others. My university students have helped me answer many of the questions I think are crucial to teaching: questions like "How many ways can you think of to read a text?" or "What can a young teacher do to make a positive first impression?" I thank them for their contributions. If you, the reader of this little book of ideas, develop other ideas that work and would like to share them, I'd love to hear from you. If you use the ideas in this book, I'd also love to hear from you about what works and what doesn't.

You can write to me at the following address:

Jim Parsons
Department of Secondary Education
3rd Floor Education South
University of Alberta
Edmonton, Alberta
T6G 2G5
Canada

# HOW TO BECOME AN EMPOWERED TEACHER

I think being a teacher is the best job in the world. Still, I'm not blind. I also know that being a teacher can, on some days, be the worst job in the world. When I first meet my undergraduate students, I ask them to consider these two questions: (1) What makes a good teacher? and (2) What keeps a good teacher going, despite the problems of teaching?

We almost always discover the same thing. There is a difference between being just a teacher and being a great teacher, being one who has the power and strength to keep on keeping on despite the problems. Recently, much has been written about empowerment. I address it in this practical book of ideas because it focuses on one of the most practical of all teaching questions: How can you grow to become a stronger teacher?

In answering this question, I have tried to draw from the research and the conversations I have had with many other teachers and students. I encourage you to ask yourself the questions outlined under the characteristics of empowerment.

## Ten Characteristics of Empowerment

*Morality*

1.  Work from an ethic.

    It's not good enough that something works. It's only good enough if it's good. There is a big difference between taking a bag of tricks into the classroom and teaching from a context of principles. Teaching is not just a group of things to do. For real empowerment to take place, there must be a fundamental ethic that grounds activity.
    - What is it that guides my teaching?
    - What is my ethical grounding?

2.  Think past the written code. It's not good enough.

    Often young student teachers wonder what their legal rights are in difficult situations. Are they allowed to stop a fight? Can they report a parent or teacher who is harming a child? The written code is the weakest of all guides on which to structure teaching behavior. While it is important to know the minimum standards for behavior, the written code is insufficient in itself to empower the actions of teachers.
    - How can I know when the written code is powerless?
    - When are the minimums insufficient for powerful action?

*Vision*

3. Establish the vision of your first love.

   Why did I want to become a teacher in the first place? What is it that will keep me teaching in spite of terrific odds, like lack of money and respect? The most important question any teacher asks and answers is this: Where do I find the joy in teaching? I believe that most teachers are, or were, visionaries. To capture and hold the vision that led you into teaching is a key to finding your joy. To carry this vision into classrooms is a key to establishing the kind of powerful relationships that teachers can build with students.
   - How can I stay in touch with the motivating power of my first love for teaching?
   - How can it guide my actions as a teacher?

4. Know yourself.

   Some people hold teaching jobs who have absolutely nothing going for them. They have neither the basic talent or skill for teaching. Quite simply, they should quit—for everyone's well-being. Fortunately, these people are small in number. Most teachers have distinctive talents, not all the same, that allow them to be quite wonderful teachers. An important teaching activity is to honestly claim both your strengths and weaknesses. Then, act on what you know.
   - What are my talents?
   - What is there about me that helps me create successful and powerful classroom experiences for kids?
   - How can I make the most of the talents I have?

*Action*

5. Make decisions that are possible to implement.

   It starts as a great idea, a dreamer's dream, a goal, a desire, a yearning. All teachers start out wanting to be good teachers, working to figure out ways to help students learn. Many find the going tough and give up. How can I turn my ideas and dreams into active reality? Although it seems almost too simple to say, there is a psychological well-being that comes from making attainable goals and feeling good when they are reached. Such action becomes an activity-celebrating orientation that encourages the growth of power by forcing people to keep trying.
   - What kinds of goals can I reach?
   - How can I use the things I have to reach them?
   - How can I overcome my own shortcomings?

6. Accept responsibility for what you know.

   We can fill ourselves so full of information that we get constipated on the things we know. To take responsibility for what we know makes all education a political activity. What we learn calls us to action. Interestingly, we also learn more (and differently) when we act on what we know (this is the meaning of the Greek term praxis).

- How does what I know affect how I live and act?
- Is it possible to know too much? too little?

7. Make a distinction between the good and the very good.

It is easy to make a distinction between the good and the bad. Most humans understand the difference. But it is often harder (and we are more easily seduced by our laziness not to try) to distinguish between the "good enough" and the "very good." The good enough is, simply, not good enough for teachers.

- What are the best activities, goals, arrangements, ideas, reactions, or justifications?
- Why are these the best?
- How can I gain the discipline to do the very best?

## Gracious Day-to-Day Living

8. Establish roots—a "family" tradition.

"We are family!" the song goes. Teachers are a unique culture, with a unique language, a unique understanding, a unique profession, a unique calling, a unique evaluation for success, and a unique reason for working.

- What are those things that make us a family, distinct from other groups?
- How can we celebrate the experience of teaching in the most powerful way?
- What can I do to build up our family?

9. Say nice things to yourself.

Inside our heads, there is a little voice that talks to us. But sometimes this voice is not very friendly. Teachers, especially, have a ruinous tendency to say nasty things to themselves. Plus, our little voices don't always keep a balanced view. One rotten decision or bad move seems to outweigh many positive actions. The answer to this problem is simple: when you can, say nice things to yourself. And keep a more honest balance sheet.

- What do I do that is good?
- How many ways can I praise my own actions?

10. If you're going to hang your head, look for money.

We all make mistakes—absolutely blow it. And when we do, we deserve to feel bad about our mistakes and disappointed in ourselves for making them. But our bad moods can't last forever. We must start to work and live again. Even in the middle of feeling bad, there are usually positive aspects that can be found. Once a positive is found, life becomes more powerful again.

- How can I learn from mistakes and grow to a richer and wiser experience?
- What can I do that will lift me above my mistakes?

# HOW TO BUILD A UNIT BY YOURSELF

One of the most important tasks teachers have is the job of creating a unit of study for their students. My experience in creating teachers' guides and units of study is that building materials for different teachers can be quite a challenge. No two teachers have exactly the same idea about what is good or what they want and can use.

Teachers are very human. The task of unit building is especially difficult because a good unit of study for one teacher is not always a good unit of study for another teacher. Teaching is done by people, all with different ideas about what is important and with a wide variety of very acceptable skills and personalities.

What all these words mean to you is that it may seem easy to pick up another teacher's unit, whether it is commercially prepared or not, and say, "Guess my work's all done!" If you have this idea, you couldn't be more wrong. You must make your own units of study. If you don't, you will never really be comfortable. You may find aces in someone else's work (and when you do, use them), but you will also find huge spaces. It's these spaces that you have to fill.

The final goal in any complete unit is to have as many great lesson plans as there are days to fill. With this goal in mind, let me offer you the following advice on how to plan a unit of study.

## Tips About Planning

1.  Whenever you are planning a unit, start fresh. You do the initial planning and structuring. Ultimately, what you believe is important becomes what's important.

2.  The following steps work for me, and I think that they are not subject-specific. (Always remember that advice is like money in the bank. It's yours to do with what you will, or will not.)

3.  Find the curriculum guide for your area. This has both legal and practical applications. Legally, you are required to teach the provincial curriculum. Practically, curriculum guides are usually full of helpful ideas. (I think too few people see their curriculum guides as a resource.) In creating units, usually the more simple you can make them, the better they are.

4. I am a concrete person. In preparing to teach a unit I break my research into two areas: content and methods. (Remember, however, that this is a contrived split for teachers. As you are actually teaching, content and method merge. But in planning, the separation between knowing and doing may simplify your work.)

5. Photocopy the part of the curriculum guide that you will be teaching. Read it carefully. As you read, selectively highlight and list the things that you believe, according to the guide, students should know after they study this unit. This is your teaching grocery list. Consider the scope of the unit. Make an initial quick decision about how important the unit is and how long it should take. If your answer is six weeks, make it a six-week unit. If it's eight weeks, make it an eight-week unit. Unless there is really a good reason, don't change your mind. If you keep wavering, you'll spend so much time trying to decide, you won't get anything done. If, after you teach a unit, you look back and see that you've made a mistake, change it for next year.

6. Look at the learning activities included in the curriculum guide. (Most teachers tend to see the curriculum guide as merely a list of content or topics. This is unfortunate. When this happens, they tend to miss what is there.) List every learning activity suggested in the curriculum guide, in no particular order. Come to think of the curriculum guide in your subject area as a resource for ideas. Again, it's "money in the bank."

7. Once you have listed both content and methods from the curriculum guide, you are ready to look at other resources. This step is where I think teachers make the most mistakes, work too hard, and become frustrated and confused. There are two mistakes I think teachers can make. First, they forget they are teaching children. Second, they believe they have to know everything before they begin to teach.

8. To find appropriate content, you need appropriate resources. I have found that 15 small sections of 15 different books on any subject are better than one dissertation on the same subject. Remember that you are working with students, not experts. (Certainly, you will want to offer students an opportunity to explore in greater depth according to their abilities. But this can be done person-to-person, by suggesting further resources to meet additional needs and desires.) To find appropriate content, spend a morning in the library. Find about ten books that each have a small 8 to 10 page section on the topic you want to teach.

   *Note:* If you find two 500-page books on the same topic, it will take you weeks to get through them. Furthermore, after you read them diligently, what will you have? You will have far more information than you can possibly use when constructing a unit of study for your students. You will have so much information you will not be able to make the content decisions you need to make. I would encourage you to read more in-depth, but not at the point of making your first unit plan.

9. After you have found the short resources and realize that someone else has done your work for you by shaping a huge mass of information into ten pages, feel grateful. Second, begin to read and take notes. As you read these resources, you will find that certain content is redundant. (Ten science books will repeat specific vocabulary, concepts, or activities on electricity, for example.) Choose about 15 to 20 things, ideas, and generalizations that these resources repeat. Your operative question is "What points of content do all the resources seem to mention?" I suggest that you never pick more than 20-25 points of content.

10. Write these 20-25 points of content in sentences on a separate piece of paper. This paper will serve you well. Essentially, this (along with the specific content from the curriculum guides you have—they should be nearly the same) becomes the core content you want your students to know when the unit is finished. You can also photocopy these sentences for students to help them prepare for tests.

11. As you are looking at your resources, especially if your subject area has activity components, look for ideas for experiments or activities that the resources recommend. List those you believe might be helpful to you. (Hint: don't miss the chance to read other people's textbooks. But remember that textbooks are written by real people like me, who often make mistakes. Don't believe they are perfect; still, they often have very good ideas, questions, and activities that the author has already completed. You can modify these for your own use.)

12. If there are other provincial resources or teaching units (teachers' guides can be very helpful) on the topic you are teaching, check them for two things: (1) stimulating activities for students and (2) crucial content that you may have missed. List anything else that might fit into your unit.

13. Taking all the material and ideas you have gathered, literally cut and paste your unit together. (Remember that this is your unit. There are times when you might want to follow another person's curriculum unit, and this is good; but you must decide what is most appropriate for your own unit.)

14. I suggest finding or making a big, current, empty calendar to jot down what will happen each day throughout the unit (something about one meter by one meter and a half is about right). I would even

encourage you to put this completed calendar up in the class so the students can see what's happening—sort of a "preview of coming attractions." Organize your unit considering the scope of the unit, the variety of activities, chronology of topics, holidays, or whatever else is important.

15. Construct a finished product that is tight, well-organized, and justifiable.

16. Let me offer some little pieces of advice I learned from my teaching:
    - Think skills. (Always work towards students learning.)
    - Think success. (Work for mastery of the content, not a quick once over.)
    - Be sensitive to students' leadings. (The statement I always tell my students is this: plans are absolute if nothing better happens in class.)
    - Ask yourself the important question: "What will the students be doing when I am doing what I am doing?" (Don't just think about what you will do. Try to imagine how the class will respond to the environment and activities you set up.)
    - Don't get upset when things don't go the way you have planned. (It is far better to fill each day with good learning activities than it is to hurry through the material.)

# HOW TO PLAN LESSONS

All teachers worth their salt know what they are going to do when they go into the classroom. They believe that without the direction that a lesson plan gives, the class would have to rely on luck for something good to happen. If you are a teacher, you know that you need lesson plans if you are to teach students. At the same time, you know that you can not be constrained by the objectives of your plans. Sometimes, particularly in subject areas (like science, social studies, and English) that prize being current and up-to-date, better things can happen than what you have planned. You must be sensitive to the possibility. As I have stated earlier, the theory I have developed to guide my work is this: lesson plans are absolutely crucial—if nothing better happens.

Below I have listed some of the things I have discovered over the years that have helped me make better lesson plans. But once again don't be so tied to your plans that you cannot be sensitive to other things that might happen.

## Hints About Planning

1. Remember that the key question in lesson planning is "What do I really want to do?" There are always at least two things that are being taught during a lesson plan. There is the content you choose and there is the way you choose to teach. You are teaching information (facts and concepts), but you are also teaching how people should interact with each other. Don't forget, your plans both introduce your students to the content and to the political and social structure of the society in which they will live. Ask: What goals do you have for your group? What general principles do you follow when you teach? How do you think people learn? should learn?

2. In lesson planning, format is an important consideration. Lesson plans take different forms, but all can be thought of in terms of the metaphor of taking a trip. I call this lesson-planning process "Driving through Chicago." I use three forms of plans. Briefly, one plan form considers the whole trip from Edmonton to Prince Edward Island. The second plan form considers where we will stop each day of the trip. The third plan form considers special difficulties (like driving through Chicago) that we will meet each day. Driving through Chicago holds some of the same pot holes that teaching holds. If I take

the southern route around the Great Lakes, I always plan to drive through Chicago on Sunday; I always prepare for the toll booths by having correct change ready; I always have a good city route pre-planned because of the constant construction; and I am always on the look-out for detours. Teaching, too, is filled with little, unexpected, and annoying situations. You must be as ready as possible.

*Hints for considering these three forms when devising unit-lesson plans.*

**Form One:** The Unit Plan (also see How to Build a Unit by Yourself)
- a) Decide how long the unit should take in the yearly scheme of things.
- b) Find or make a big calendar that shows the days. (You will want to write short notes in the day spaces.)
- c) Rough in all the activities (formal evaluations, research days, reviews, movies or media, tried-and-true lesson ideas).
- d) Look for special considerations of the school calendar that would disrupt your plans. These include things like report card days, Christmas, civic holidays, and field trips. Then, change things to fit your work around these disruptions.

**Form Two:** The Daily Agenda
- a) Review your unit plan, looking for poor decisions. Change things right now. (It's work and your tendency will be to want to put it off, but experience will teach you that it's far easier to change things now than later.)
- b) Consider variety of activity. Make sure that you have included lots of different types of activities. Remember my "manna from heaven" theory: even the food you love the most becomes sickening when it's the only thing you have to eat.
- c) Determine not to cheat. (Hint: do it once, and do it right!) Write your plans completely, and write them with a mind's eye for next year. (If you work now, you can relax later.)
- d) If my family were planning a trip to Prince Edward Island, we would plan carefully where to stay each night. Our goal was to hit every hotel with a large swimming pool or a water slide. Don't forget: it's almost as important where you stop as where you start.

**Form Three:** The Lesson Plan
- a) Review the form of your plan. Reread the plan checking for things you don't understand. (If possible, find a critical friend who can tell you what can't be understood. You may remember tomorrow what you wrote tonight; but, if you are like me, you will be a stranger to your own thinking next year. You must take the extra moments now to save the extra hours next year. If you don't, you will find yourself in my situation as a second-year teacher. I had to virtually re-plan all my activities.

b) Make sure you write your plan so that you can follow it when you teach. Consider your enterprise. You have to be able to work in front of the "traffic" and the group. Good spacing of your notes helps you. Numbers are easier to follow than dashes. Colored highlighters also help you see where you are more quickly. Be smart. Help yourself use your own plan.

3. Lesson plans encompass what you believe is crucial to education. For example, I believe that because people learn better from active involvement, I should involve people in the learning. So I work to build classes where students are active.

When making a plan, I think it is important to know the content of the plan as well as what you want to do. Because I believe there should be activity involved, I always ask the question: What are the students going to be doing when I am doing what I'm doing? There are some other important questions involved here.

a) Can I keep control of the situation? (If not, don't do it!)

b) What do the students like? (Choose activities students appreciate.)

c) What have we done before? ((Don't repeat activities over and over again.)

d) What, from my experience, won't work? (If it won't work with a particular group, don't do it.)

e) What are the personalities of the specific people in this group? And then what? (For example, don't put two disruptive personalities together in the same group.)

f) What do I enjoy doing personally? (If you like a particular activity, chances are that enthusiasm will spread to your students.)

g) What do I believe about teaching students? (For me, self-esteem is important; success breeds success; activity, good directions, bite-size pieces are helpful.)

4. Lesson plans consider the curriculum. Let the curriculum guide you are legally constrained to use help you plan the lessons you choose to teach. This guide will probably contain a list of knowledge, skills, and attitudes sections that are, in themselves, wonderfully rich in hints for making up lesson plans. To repeat, there are two reasons for knowing the curriculum. First, it is the legal tender of the profession. Second, if it is like most I have read, it offers practical ideas for teaching. Sometimes these ideas are hard to find, but here's my hint: look for verbs. Design activities that mimic the objectives of the curriculum.

5. Timing is a key point. A principle I follow is to never give enough time for kids to be finished. It is easier to extend time and look nice than cut down time and look mean. Dead space can be a killer.

## General Hints About Teaching and Planning

1.  I always try to work from two important beliefs: (1) Students want to learn; they just don't want to be bored. (2) Young people have a unique sense of fair play.

2.  Earning the right to be heard is a key to teaching at any level. Model behavior. The research repeatedly suggests two points: (1) students want to like their teachers and (2) they want to learn. Expect hard work from your students. If they like you, they will usually work to please you. Teachers often make the mistake of believing that kids will like them if they squander gifts and charity (something for nothing) on them. My experience, and it comes from having made mistakes, is that constantly receiving something for nothing erodes self-motivation and steals the student's soul. It puts out both the fire in the heart and the fire in the belly.

3.  In my experience, projects are a key tool. Projects give students something to rally around. They also foster group identity. Also, don't be afraid to involve the affective in teaching. (Note: Research suggests that Grade 8 students are the most pro-active and altruistic of all students. If a project includes doing something nice for someone else, there can't be a better feeling or lesson.)

4.  Here's another principle that guides my work: all education has a political agenda. Knowledge is worth knowing if it improves the world. Ask: now that we have learned something from this lesson, how then should we live?

# HOW TO TALK THE TALK LIKE A PRO

Have you ever had the following thought? If teaching is a profession, it should be like other professions. There should be an esoteric lingo that teachers can speak just to confuse those who are not teachers! Or maybe this has already happened. Perhaps you have walked into the staff room or attended the latest conference only to be overwhelmed by what seems to be a new language you have never heard before, that seems to be the latest rage. You hate to admit it, but you don't know what these new terms mean. The speaker talks about global education. Does this mean that someone is taking students to Europe? Or that the school is getting into "total management." Will you still have a job? You just figured out last year's terms, eg., inquiry learning and now this year's terms are being introduced.

You know you're a good teacher. You can "walk the walk." Still, it bothers you because you can't "talk the talk." If you pick up the latest copy of a journal in your subject, you only partly understand it. Are you a mind-mapping, cooperative learner? Have you been self-esteemed? Which hemisphere of your brain is dominant? Is any part of your brain working at all?

Have you been confused by terms? If so, don't feel you're alone. Even those in the field of education have a hard time keeping up with the language. What can you do?

Here's my five-step advice for keeping up with the latest in educational jargon. Doing this activity might not make you a better teacher; but then again, you just never know what good ideas you might find in a book or journal article. When you have finished, you will talk the talk as well as any pro.

## Five Steps to a More Clearly Esoteric Professional Teaching Vocabulary

**Step One:** The first thing to do is to relax. Remember that education is like any other profession. The vocabulary is constantly changing. But like most professions, the basic ideas remain very much the same.

**Step Two:** Listen to other teachers (especially professors in faculties of education) talk. If you listen long enough, you will come to one conclusion. They don't know what they are talking about! Go back and read Step One: Relax!

**Step Three:** Make a pact with a small number of other teachers to really talk about education. (I say a small number, because the larger the number the more difficult to keep your conversation from falling into the realm of gossip.) These discussions should include talking about your job, but they require some sensitivity when speaking about the kids in your class, their parents, or your particular administration.

I'm not suggesting that you eliminate shop talk. That would be impossible, plus it would dispense with those moments of good therapy you need to continue the job. But I am suggesting that you find some people who are like-minded about educational issues and who want to spend some time discussing the enduring problems of the profession. Don't think you have to be in a university class to discuss educational topics. (You may even find that a reading-discussion group would be a good focus for your small group.)

**Step Four:** Read (or re-read) some of the educational classics. These are the essays or books that were included in bibliographies that were all-too-long, or you were all-too-busy-for when you were an undergraduate student. Or if you are an undergraduate student, these are the readings you skipped over when you learned they were not going to be on the final exam. You will find that some educational ideas remain valid forever. Your readings will help you center on these. For example, fads come and go, but students are still asking and answering questions.

**Step Five:** Try to keep up with the current ideas in teaching. Once a year, take a two-day vacation to the university education library nearest to you. When you get there, head immediately to the Current Index to Journals in Education (CIJE). Pick a topic you're interested in, and look it up in the index. From the abstracts, pick some articles that look interesting.

From the pile of articles you have gathered, pick the most promising. Keep reading only those articles that are the most interesting. As you read, start taking notes. You will find that some educational ideas seem to come and go.

Create a glossary of educational terms that are currently "hot" in education. Don't be surprised if you don't recognize some of the terms, but do recognize the definitions. Educational jargon is just like everything else. Sometimes simple and good ideas sound even better if they are dressed up with a fancy name. Try to learn about the idea, not just how to say and define the word. Definitions are only simplifications of the ideas, like saying that Edmonton is a city in Canada. It helps you know something about Edmonton, but it doesn't mean that there isn't more you can learn by living in Edmonton. Try to learn as much as you can about the things that interest you. Remember, learning is supposed to be fun — not a chore. If it doesn't interest you, skip it.

**Step Six:** As a final task, pick a small number of vocabulary terms that fit your subject area or beliefs best and that you believe you will find a good use for. Write them down and commit them to memory. Then, whenever the need arises, use these terms. Not only have you learned to talk the current talk, there's a chance you will have found something worthwhile in the journals that you can use.

# HOW TO WRITE A POSITION PAPER

Writing position papers allows students to gain a greater voice in their work. Position papers are powerful activities because they help students synthesize the information they have learned around a decision they have made. They are also useful evaluations for teachers because they allow a teacher to see how students are understanding the material they are being confronted with, to evaluate writing skills and the ability to justify using evidence, and to come to know students a little more personally. An added benefit is that position papers can be more provocative and more fun to read than a typical "review what you have learned" essay question.

A position paper usually calls for a personal response to a situation or issue. It works best when the issue in question means something to the person responding. While it is possible to write an academic position paper about some little-known historical situation, teachers usually get a better response from students when they choose an issue that is known to the responder. The type of writing called for is personal, pointed, and works best if some passion can be generated. The evidence called for is not to be found in a libraried collection from antiquity. It is to be found in the head and heart of the person writing.

## How to Set Up a Position Paper

1.  Obviously, in setting out to structure a position paper assignment, it is best to find an issue worth talking about. This means finding or creating an issue where there are at least two sides that can be supported as a best choice.

2.  When introducing the topic I want students to write about, I usually try to be evocative. That is, I try to set up a position paper by writing a short problem-story about a person involved in the center of the issue. If there is a legitimate possibility, I try to stir some emotion by finding and writing about an example where some harm has come to a person who is either naive or innocent. If possible, I try to extend the problem in one way or another to an extreme. I don't worry too much about overstatement. In fact, I've found that overstatement can really help get things stirred up a bit. My goal is to get the emotions stirred, or at least force the student to recognize that there might be a problem that ought to be addressed.

3.  After settling on the topic, another practical concern is setting directions for the position paper. I work hard to create clear directions. And I write them very carefully. (Hint: I encourage you to write all your directions in a step-by-step manner. I believe students should be able to follow the directions, if they need to, in a linear manner. Most students will know exactly what to do, but there are always some who will not.) Directions should attempt to help everyone understand just "what the teacher wants." Students will ask this same question over and over: "What do you want?" Creating clear, easy-to-follow directions will help eliminate some of these questions.

4.  Before giving the assignment to students, the final step is to follow your own directions and write the assignment yourself. Generally, doing the assignment will only prove that you have done a wonderful, almost ingenious, job creating the lesson plan. However, sometimes writing an assignment will help you find fatal flaws in your work. Even the best teachers can get too close to their work and create assignments that students find difficult to answer. Testing the assignment will eliminate sentences that cannot be understood or directions that are incomprehensible.

The following is an example of a position paper that I might use with my class. Note how the directions are set out in a step-by-step format.

## An Example of a Position Paper Assignment: Advertising

**Directions:** Below you will read about a problem caused by advertising. As you read, consider the issue and jot down any points that come into your head. Then, reread the assignment. Before you write, jot down a few simple points that ought to be included in your work.

When you write your position paper, take a position that expresses how you feel about the issue question. Make sure to include the things you already know about the issue as evidence to support your point. Remember to state your position clearly at the beginning of your paper.

In this issue, you will see problems that North Americans must face as they look to the future. This is only one issue, but it shows some of the decisions that people in modern society must consider. Most choices are complex and must be considered carefully. Beliefs about what is a quality life, what is the nature of individual rights and freedoms, and how people should be treated are the foundation of all choices.

Consider the issue and the choices it asks you to make. At the foundation of the choice you make are important questions you must answer. What kind of lifestyle do you support? What social, economic, spiritual, and physical considerations must be made if you and your society are going to enjoy the quality of life that you believe is important? These are some of the questions you must answer as you choose among the alternatives presented by this issue. If you think of other important questions, write these at the end of your paper.

## ISSUE : SHOULD ADVERTISING BE STRICTLY CONTROLLED?

Christmas morning comes and little Mary is thrilled. The toys she saw on television and wanted so much are under the tree. Santa was good. New Year's morning comes. Mom and Dad are angry. The Christmas toys that Mary so desperately wanted haven't been played with in days. What happened?

Advertising is big business for business. Businesses advertise to sell their products. When advertising is done right, it can benefit consumers. The main purpose of advertising is to tell consumers the value of products and explain how products can be used to benefit the consumer. Because different consumers have different needs, advertising can help consumers make more considerate choices among several alternatives.

But advertising can deceive as well. Sometimes producers use seductive ad campaigns that tell little about the product but are so cleverly made that they persuade nevertheless. Some ads are meant to appeal to the emotions of the consumer rather than the consumer's ability to reason. By using camera angles, stimulating music, and high-tech video some television advertisements appear to downright lie to consumers. They make things seem bigger, better, or faster than they actually are.

Children are easy targets. Usually children are the most easily persuaded by seductive advertising. Around Christmastime, particularly, television ads provide a virtual festival of Christmas dreams—all dancing in the heads of children. They almost encourage children to beg their parents for toys that parents either can't afford or don't want to buy. Young children are impressionable and self-centered. Family stress can be created when ads encourage children to play "gimme" and force thoughtful parents to say "no."

Even if children can persuade their parents to buy them the toys they seem to want so desperately, there might be other problems. Sometimes ads make toys seem better than they actually are. Children can be easily disappointed when toys don't live up to their advance billing. Parents can become disillusioned and upset with their kids when they have spent hard-earned money on toys that are opened with glee on Christmas morning and are collecting dust by New Year's Day.

How should advertising be dealt with? Because there are both benefits and problems, advertising provides a dilemma for both producers and consumers. Throughout the book, a number of examples have been given that might help you reach a considered decision about advertising. Review these. You may want to find other evidence that can help you make up your mind in magazines or newspaper articles. When you have collected and considered the evidence, write a position paper answering the question: "Should advertising be strictly controlled?"

*Note:* This example is just one of the myriad issues that could fire up your students. My attempt was to highlight the directions, the tone of the short focus question, and the setting of the issue question.

# HOW TO KEEP TRACK OF MOVIES AND AV MATERIALS

## RATIONALE

One of the important lessons of teaching is that a little extra work in the first place can save a lot of extra work in the second place. Some teachers learn the lesson early, some by making and correcting mistakes as they work, and some never learn it. I must admit, it took me two years of redoing the same work over and over again until I finally caught on to this truth.

Movies can add much to your classes, but they must be used correctly — not just as a time-filler. My method of keeping track of movies or other audio-visual materials has two aspects. First, how can you keep a systematic record of movies that you review or use? Second, how can you help students attend to information in the movies they are viewing in class? Ideas for creating generic black-line masters are provided that will help you do both.

It almost goes without saying that teachers need to keep a record of the movies and audio-visual materials they preview or use. My encouragement is simply to make taking notes a habit. When you are previewing a movie (need I state the absolute necessity for previewing movies before you show them?), always have paper and pen ready to record some general notes.

It is always a surprise to watch teachers (especially student teachers) show a movie without giving students a set of focus questions to help them attend to what they are watching. The focus questions not only give the students something to look for, but they also serve a management function. When the lights grow dim in your classroom, it does not have to signal an invitation to a party. Focus questions also serve as both a note-collecting tool to review after the movie is finished and as a review sheet for later exams.

*Note:* Specific focus questions are best for helping students view movies and other audio-visual materials. Questions matching the chronology of the movie or audio-visual material work especially well. My experience is that if students get confused or miss things that go by, they tend to quit caring. But easy questions that they can wait for and quickly answer, encourage the students to continue the assignment.

Don't make your focus questions too difficult. Although specific questions are best, a generic sheet like Sheet B (which follows) can help. It is better than no sheet at all. You can use it as a guide to develop specific questions.

Sheet A is for your record keeping. Sheet B is a generic sheet you can use to help students take notes when viewing a movie or other audio-visual material.

24

## Sheet A: Movie Record-Keeping Sheet

Name: _____ Length: _____

1.  What is the movie/video/film about?_____
    _____
    _____

2.  What is the movie/video/film really about? _____
    _____
    _____

3.  How can I use it in class? _____
    _____
    _____

    a. Grade Level: _____Class:_____Topic: _____
    b. Timing considerations:_____
    c. Ideas for use _____
    _____

    d. Specific Questions I Can Ask/Assignment Ideas _____
    _____
    _____

    e. Other considerations (Suitability, Understandability, Currency,
       Tolerance and Understanding, etc.) _____
    _____

4.  Notes about teaching the movie _____
    _____

    a. As a teacher, what questions could I ask of the movie to help me
       discuss the movie after it is finished? List two questions.
       _____
       _____

    b. Where could I go from here? List three possibilities for follow-up
       activities.
       _____
       _____
       _____

    c. Evaluate the movie. Would I use it? Why or why not?
       _____
       _____
       _____

## Sheet B: Questions for Viewing/Discussing a Movie

1. What is this movie about? (Write a two-sentence summary of the movie.) _____

   _____

   _____

2. Movies are generally either art or documentary.
   Which kind was this? _____
   Why do you know? _____

   _____

   _____

3. What scenes/pictures stand out in your mind as you view this movie? _____

   _____

   _____

   Why do you think they stand out? _____

   _____

   _____

4. List five things that are important to remember from this movie. In other words, what do you think you, or other people should remember after the movie is completed? (Take rough notes on a separate piece of paper and choose five things from these rough notes.)
   a.) _____
   b.) _____
   c.) _____
   d.) _____
   e.) _____

5. Does this movie prompt action. Does it makes suggestions about what people should do? Can you infer possible need for actions? If so, what actions?

   _____

   _____

   _____

   _____

   _____

   _____

   _____

# HOW TO WRITE QUESTIONS FOR READINGS

Educational fads may come and go, but asking and answering questions remains one of the truly fundamental activities of all education. Unfortunately, many of the questions you find in student and teacher materials are duds. First, they often ask for narrow responses that encourage students to find only the facts in the reading. Factual questions are important, but they also tend to be boring, tedious, and encourage students to assume the stance of a passive learner. Second, few questions in professionally published materials seem to encourage students to move to "higher-level" (the term higher-level is taken from Bloom's Taxonomy) activities. The shame is that most published texts and guides never take advantage of what students could (and want to) do if they were challenged.

Here's a hint about creating questions. Almost everyone in education has seen Bloom's Taxonomy of Higher and Lower-level questions. If you don't remember it, find a basic educational text and photocopy the taxonomy. Basic educational texts seem to follow an educational belief that elevates higher-order questions to the highest priority while ignoring lower-order questions. This trend probably exists because, for too many years, only lower-order questions seemed to be asked by teachers. Higher-order questions were virtually ignored.

The truth is that both higher and lower questions are helpful and should be used. First, lower-order questions provide an opportunity to bring all students together at a beginning level of understanding. If your class is like most classes, it has students with a wide variety of abilities. Some students are way ahead and would understand the reading quite easily. Others will not. Answering factual questions helps everyone understand what is being said.

But lower-order questions are not enough. Good readings and questions should be provocative. They should be interesting. They should also allow students to explore, to question, to be critical, to build hypotheses, to evaluate, to make tentative decisions, to support points, and so on.

Here's a hint about creating good questions. The number of questions is important. Too few makes it seem that the reading is either not important or that the questions demand long answers. Too many questions tend to seem overwhelming and scare students off. My experience is that five questions is about right. Of course, the number of questions depends on the length and depth of the reading. It would also be good to encourage at least one question where students work together in groups.

## A Sample Reading with Questions

*Sniffy the Rat*

Ideas and beliefs differ among people within society. Even the impending death of vermin can cause the beliefs of people to come into conflict. Such was the case of Sniffy the Rat.

Rick Gibson was a 38-year-old Vancouver artist. For the sake of art, Gibson planned to kill a rat by dropping a 25-kilogram concrete block on the animal. While no one likes rats, Gibson's plans drew threats about a possible riot from animals lovers. The Vancouver Humane Society said that it would rescue Sniffy from death, by force if necessary. Other calls to save the rat came from as far away as Southern Ontario.

Gibson the artist remained unmoved. But Vancouver police were worried. They thought Gibson's exhibit would start a riot. "If Sniffy had a choice between a concrete block crushing him quickly and painlessly, or slowly being swallowed by a snake, I think he'd choose me. The rat was going to die anyway." Gibson bought Sniffy from a pet store that used live rats to feed to its pet snakes.

One Vancouver art critic noted that the public reaction was part of Gibson's project. If a society were extremely tolerant and an artist killed a rat on the public square, society would say "So what?" It would be meaningless, and the artist wouldn't need to do it. As an artist, she continued, Gibson depends on the public reaction.

What do you think: does Gibson's art work prove how intolerant our society really is?

*Questions:*

1.  Particular events might be analyzed in two possible ways: what is happening in a narrow sense (the particular facts of the event), and what is happening in a broad sense (the general meaning of the event). Look at the reading about Gibson and Sniffy the Rat from both the narrow and the broad sense. What do you think was happening?

2.  The reading doesn't mention what happened to Sniffy the Rat. What do you think happened? Can you find out? (Hint: Sniffy was supposed to be killed on January 6, 1989, in Vancouver.)

3.  Whose side would you take in this controversy? Why?

4.  What does the controversy show about society? Does what happened with Sniffy the Rat suggest that civilized people must learn to tolerate even the strangest behavior? Why or why not?

5.  Agree or disagree with the following statement: Beliefs about what is acceptable behavior differ in society.

## Now It's Your Turn

Directions: Below you will see two different readings, each around the 500 word mark. What they lack are good, challenging student questions. Your task as a teacher is to create five solid questions for each reading.

### READING ONE: LIVING IN A MATERIAL WORLD

Do you know the popular singer Madonna? Is she still popular? Have you seen her music videos? If so, you may realize that Madonna's music videos are a technology that your parents didn't have when they were kids. But one of them, "Material Girl," represents more than just a new technology. It represents a new morality, a new kind of spirit, and a new way of understanding the world. It's not the skimpy outfits or the new dance steps that highlight this new way of thinking about the world. It's the words or lyrics of her song. When she says, "I am a material girl. I live in a material world," she clearly states one of the changes in modern lifestyles and modern values.

When this reading was being written, Madonna was the most popular singer around. But you may not have heard of Madonna. Her popularity may have faded and she may now be a "nobody." If so, she also represents a change in what we believe is important. Andy Warhol, a pop-artist and social critic from New York City, stated that in our new age of fast-paced technological change everybody would become famous, but just for 15 minutes. What he meant was that the values that made people famous in the past, for instance a John A. MacDonald, a Norman Bethune, or a Laura Secord, are being replaced by a different value system and a different way of being famous.

Today, to become famous a person doesn't have to be heroic or live a life filled with noted public service. Instead, this traditional idea of fame has been replaced by the idea of being a celebrity. Like the singing group Millie Vanilli, becoming a celebrity is sometimes more a matter of deceit than work. It may seem that almost anyone can become a celebrity, if they are odd enough, loud enough, pretty enough, or rich enough. Unfortunately, even when someone truly deserves fame, we often tend to forget them quickly.

If what Andy Warhol says is true, why is it true? Why is our modern society willing to replace heroes with celebrities? Why do some people seem to burst on the scene quickly and just as quickly, disappear from view? Do we have such short memories? Part of the answer might have to do with the media technologies that we have and use. Part of the answer might lie with new values we have adopted.

### *READING TWO: HOW DOES THE MEDIA IN A FAST-PACED SOCIETY CHANGE OUR VALUES?*

Television and radio use a hit-and-run mentality. Things come and go before we know it. Young people are bombarded with sights and sounds—all new, all different, all coming quickly and then just as quickly disappearing. A successful television show is one that lasts more than a year. A successful Top 40 hit is one that stays on the charts for three weeks. Media technology has the ability to stimulate our senses quickly, to encourage us to buy, and then to make us believe that what we just bought is no longer good enough.

One example of this ability is in the sale of computers. If you have recently bought a computer, you will know how confusing the whole process can be. First, you realize that computer technology is constantly changing and improving. As these improvements are made, the product is also becoming less expensive. The machine you can buy today for $1500 is far superior to the machine you could buy just last year for the same amount of money. You have a dilemma: when should you buy?

Second, the ads in computer magazines and stores are seductive. They promise that the new machines are far superior to the machines that were just on the market. Have you ever noticed? They only ask you questions you can answer "yes" to. Don't you want the best that money can buy?

You carefully plan, and then you decide to buy. You are happy because your new computer performs all the functions the company promised. But here's the problem. If you are to stay satisfied with what you bought, don't read the computer advertisements. They will only tell you how bad a deal you got.

Your computer is obsolete! It is no longer the best you could buy. It can't do what the new computers can do. You feel bad because you don't have the newest and best. You forget the things your computer does well, and think of all the things it can't do.

You have been seduced by advertising. The best ads make you feel unsatisfied with what you have and make you believe that you can be satisfied only if you have the new and improved version. If it can make you feel bad enough or unsatisfied, you might just buy again.

### Part B: Directions

You have read these short readings and have designed questions for each of these readings. It's easy to write your own reading. Pick an issue that is important to your subject area. Make your reading speak to your students. Keep it short, about 500 words. Then write five questions or so that will highlight the parts of the reading you think are important. Remember to save all your work from year to year.

# HOW TO MAKE A FINAL EXAM

Comprehensive exams are powerful learning tools and I encourage their use. Let me give you some reasons why.

First, exams give teachers a real idea of how their students are doing. Second, through the process of creating a comprehensive exam, teachers decide what content is worth knowing. A comprehensive exam serves as a personal guide for designing teaching plans. Third, a comprehensive exam helps students focus on what they are doing in class. If students know that a comprehensive exam waits for them sometime soon, most will attend to the activities of the classroom in a more rigorous manner.

But there are a couple of good reasons for using exams that might seem new. I find that a comprehensive exam, when students do well, provides a real sense of success and accomplishment. Furthermore, the longer and harder the comprehensive exam, the more students feel they have accomplished when (not if!) they complete it successfully.

As I became a more experienced teacher, one of my main tasks became helping students do well on their exams. This one task helped change the relationship between teacher and student in my class. Very quickly I was on the side of the students and out of a conflict situation with them. We worked together to "beat" the curriculum content and the test.

Once I discovered how well gaming activities and other reviews worked to review the material that students were supposed to learn, helping students do well became much easier. My spoken contract with students was that they had to do only two things: to come and to care. My job was to teach. We went over and over the material until the students knew it. Then I gave them a comprehensive exam.

When students had done well on their comprehensive tests, I would send the completed and graded exam home with students for a parent to sign and send back. Teachers in my past wanted my parents to sign my tests, but for very different reasons. I think they wanted to show my parents how terrible I was doing and wanted to terrorize me into working harder.

But my plan was more gentle and probably more devious. I wanted to show off to parents. First I wanted them to know that in my class their kids were working hard and that I was teaching vast amounts of content. Second, I wanted them to know that in my class their kids were being extremely successful on the very difficult and comprehensive exams I was making.

Early in my teaching career, I had theorized that there was a success cycle at work in schools. I came to realize that I had watched a lack-of-success cycle work all too well. I felt that there might be another dimension, the reverse if you will. If students experienced a little success, they might find out it felt good. I believed that this feeling of success would encourage them to work just a little harder to have more success—just because they liked the idea of feeling good. Like Adam Smith, I believed that people worked to maximize their own self-interest. And to a student, what would be more in their self-interest than feeling good about themselves?

My junior high teaching experience showed me that, generally, my theory worked. Over my junior high school teaching career, a large number of parents told me how surprised and pleased they were that their kids were learning so much. When students did well I was able to give them good marks on their report cards. The kids liked this; their parents liked this; and when the administration of my school complained about my marks (inferring that I was grading too easy), I showed them the comprehensive exam and encouraged them to take it. They soon left me alone with my classes.

For these reasons I have included suggestions about how to review material (both knowledge and skills) and how to use comprehensive exams. This section of the book provides a variety of evaluation types, both with the idea of Quick Quizzes and review exercises.

I believe that giving students a large final exam does not punish them for their lack of knowledge, but allows them to show how much they have learned. The redundancy offered in the activities throughout this book will, I hope, help you teach and help your students learn important knowledge. One hint about comprehensive exams. To get the students ready for the exam, teachers should review and review (in the most enjoyable ways possible) the material they consider most important.

I found that the real key was to get the students so ready for the exam that any student who paid attention in class did well. Sadly, I believe the concept of hoping that students do well on exams is not universal among teachers or administrators. Your students have probably already been in classes where exams have been made purposely difficult and taken without adequate teaching and review. The result? Students did poorly on exams and, if the experience of doing poorly is repeated, the result is that students will become frustrated and quit.

Many students have experienced this lack of success already. They may not trust teachers very much. The result is that it will take you some time to get this philosophy off the ground. The students may not trust you. Be prepared to do much of the initial work yourself. But if you ever trusted any comment in this book, trust this one: the results of helping your students do well on exams, both in terms of student learning and class atmosphere and management will be worth it!

I offer these suggestions about comprehensive exams both as an ethical way to teach (it does not prejudice slow learners like many systems) and as a practical way to work (the class responds cooperatively). My experience has been that when students take "the biggest test they have ever seen" and do very well, they increase not only their self-esteem but also their willingness to work harder the next time. I believe that good teaching and good learning go hand-in-hand. Students should have the chance to earn good grades.

I encourage you, in every unit you teach, to create a large exam of your own design as a final review of students' knowledge. To do this you might choose from the questions at the end of the chapters, from the review exercises and activities placed in the teacher's guides you use, and from the quick quizzes you design.

The following points should be followed when constructing exams.

## Point 1: Decide Between Objective (Short Answer) Exams and Subjective (Essay) Exams

Each type of exam has its good and bad points. An objective test, if students have reviewed the material well and are not thrown off by the form (sometimes teachers can make the form of an objective exam so difficult that even students who know the material can not answer the exam correctly), is generally easier for all students. Essay exams tend to favor students who are more intelligent (who think in the higher-level ways more prized in school situations—analysis, synthesis, and evaluation) and have better writing skills.

For teachers, either type of exam tends to require the same amount of work. The question is: when do you want to do the work, now or later? Objective exams are front-heavy. They take a lot of time up-front, but are relatively easy to grade. The good point is that you can save the exam (or question bank if you have a computer) from one year to the next and cut down on your work next year. An essay exam is simple to make, but takes countless hours to grade. And it doesn't get easier to grade year after year.

The level of your students makes a difference in the kind of exams you can give. Junior high students need to learn how to put their thoughts into words, but they are also working harder setting a basic core of understandings. To rely solely on essay exams would be to miss the need to develop this set of understandings. Senior high students are learning to rely more on their own ability to decide and to justify their decisions. To rely solely on objective exams would be to miss their need to develop these skills. Still the difference is not as great as most people believe. However, it does exist and should be considered. The bottom line is that there seem to be good reasons to give both types of exam questions (objective and essay) at all levels.

## Point 2: Choose Different Types of Questions for Objective Tests

Many kinds of questions might be used in a final, comprehensive exam. Each has its good and bad points.

### Type 1: Fill-in-the-Blank

Fill-in-the-blank questions provide sentences where students fill-in the appropriate word that completes each sentence. Because the word is not provided, fill-in-the-blank questions make it difficult for students to guess. They also work well because they allow students to answer the question within the context of a larger sentence. Students who have a difficult time reading and spelling can have troubles with fill-in questions; and, if a teacher takes off marks for spelling, students with poor language skills can have a tough time. One way to make the questions easier and provide spelling and answer clues is to provide a word pool below the questions for students to choose from. This move, however, changes the question into a matching-type question.

Fill-in questions are easy to create. However, they should be used only with the most important information in the unit. If they are used with less important information, students may have too tough a time. Fill-in questions work especially well with terms, definitions, and specific content facts.

*Example:*

1.  The short novel *A Christmas Carol* was written by _____ _____ to show, in part, the problems and changes of the Industrial Revolution.
    *Answer:* Charles Dickens

### Type 2: Multiple Choice

Multiple-choice questions usually provide a stem with a number of alternatives from which a student chooses the completion. The questions might be very easy (a simple definition); more difficult (where more than one answer is correct and students have to choose the best alternative); or very difficult (where students must infer a great deal from the text).

*Examples:*
*(Easy)*

1.  The study of animals (including humans) is called
    a. zoology
    b. biology
    c. botony
    d. animalology

*(More Difficult)*

2.  Which of the following helped the Japanese people gain a stronger feeling of nationalism?
    a. Japan's isolation from the rest of the world
    b. the success of Japanese sports industries

c. the need to sacrifice personal pleasure in order to industrialize

d. a and c

e. all of the above

f. none of the above

*(Difficult)*

3.  Which of the following changes in family relationships are brought about by the media? (In the space below the question, support any answers you choose.)

a. Families become more isolated.

b. Families don't stay at home much.

c. Families become less friendly.

d. Children live with their families longer.

e. Children become more difficult for their parents to handle.

Test experts suggest that multiple-choice questions are good questions because, if they are made well, they are highly correlated to a student's knowledge. They do allow for guessing, but are not as biased against students with poor language skills as fill-in-the-blank questions.

### Type Three: True or False

In True-or-False questions, students are asked to read a statement and tell whether that statement is either true or false. If students know the information, distinguishing between a true and a false statement is usually easy. If the student does not know the information, the result is a flip of the coin. The student has, theoretically, a 50–50 chance. Teachers can make True-or-False questions more difficult by asking students to tell why a false statement is false.

True-or-False questions encourage students to read questions carefully. Often students can be careless. They see two aspects of a question and jump to a conclusion. Here is an example:

_____In 1853, Commodore Matthew Perry became the first person from the Western world to fly into the airport at Tokyo.

In this question, a careless student might see both Matthew Perry and 1853 and maybe miss the fact that he sailed into the harbor and did not fly into the airport.

True-or-False questions are easy to construct and quick to grade. My encouragement is to discourage cheating by asking students to write the entire word (True or False) rather than put T or F.

### Type Four: Matching Questions

Matching questions work well for people, dates and events, and vocabulary terms and definitions. They usually have little context and are quick evaluations for important nouns (people, places, or things). I use matching because I can cover important vocabulary terms and grade the questions quickly.

Matching can be difficult, especially if your form is poor. I have found that matching questions should be created in sections (limited to one page), with no more than 25 terms in a section. More terms than this can confuse the students. You can discourage the situation where the last few matches are freebies by adding extra choices to the list of possible definitions on the right. Order each line from left to right so that the space is first, the term is second, and the letter and definition to be matched is on the far right. It makes the questions much easier to grade with a key. Make sure that the words and choices are well mixed.

*Hint #1:* Matching can be tricky for students because there is a lack of context for the answers. As you grade an exam, watch for the way students answer all the questions—but especially the matching. My experience with matching is that, on almost every test I designed, more than one answer was correct for at least one choice. I soon learned to try my best to make the matching answers discrete, but I also learned not to worry too much. I had to allow both choices to be correct.

If I caught my error quickly enough, I could go back and change the answer key to include both correct choices. However, if I was well into the test before I saw the problem, I would grade the exam according to the answers on my key. Then, I would add an extra point to everyone's exam, regardless of whether they missed the test question or not. (I never had a complaint over my procedure. In fact, by adding a single point on a very large exam, I made some students very happy.) My grading of exams was based on the theory that students should not have to pay for my mistakes. I believe this practice helped me set a positive classroom attitude and avoid being labelled as unfair. It was also good for students to learn that making an error is not the end of the world.

*Hint #2:* Watch how students, especially your hard-working ones, answer questions. They can often highlight problems in the construction of your exam. And don't worry too much. No matter how hard you work, you will always make a mistake here and there. Making a mistake is not as big a problem as most young teachers think. Students are very forgiving if they know that you have their best interests at heart.

Example of a Matching Question (Horizontal Slice of Test Page)

\_\_\_\_\_ high tech          (m) made at home

\_\_\_\_\_ cottage industry   (n) a manufacturing process in which processes are performed by machinery and electronic devices

### Type Five: Short Answer

Short-answer questions can vary from having students write objective definitions to having them subjectively justify or support points from an argument. Short-answer questions give students a structure for answering, but allow them more freedom in these answers. Short answer questions are best used for concepts that are difficult to place in a shorter form and those times when a teacher wants to minimize guessing by students.

Short-answer questions are relatively easy to grade and to design. They offer teachers an opportunity to judge a student's ability to reason or to synthesize information. They encourage students to offer more complete answers.

Here's an example of a short-answer question:

1.  As you have learned, hundreds of years ago fairy tales were told to instruct children about how to behave. Choose one of the fairy tales we have studied. In a one-paragraph summary, review the fairy tale. In your review, point out how the fairy tale instructed the children for whom it was told.

## Point 3: Take Care to Use Clear Directions

Directions are often taken for granted by teachers who are quite test-wise. However, teachers should not assume that students are as test-wise as teachers. For example, a teacher might write a question like "Should the federal government support dictatorships in the Middle East?" fully intending that students address the question "Why?" But, unless the teacher writes the question "Why?" at the end of the first question, it is not reasonable to assume that students should or will address the "Why?" part of the question. Given the way the question is written, a student is justified in answering either "yes" or "no."

At the same time, good directions help guide students' time through a test. For example, note the difference between the following questions. They both ask the same question, but the second question places a structure and a limit on the questions and gives better directions to students.

> **Question 1:** Why is wheat an important crop on the Canadian prairies?
>
> **Question 2:** In no more than four sentences, list two reasons why wheat is an important crop in the economy of Western Canada.

Directions can encourage students to attend to certain points in the question. For example, here's a good set of directions for True-and-False questions:

Read the following statements. If the statement is true, write true in the space to the left of the question number. If it is false, write false in the space to the left of the question number. If the statement is false, give a one-sentence reason why it is false. Read each statement carefully. Make sure that you don't fall for any of my trick questions.

## Point 4: Take the Exam Yourself Before Giving It to Students

No teacher should ever give an exam without taking it first. Better yet, ask a teacher friend to take it. Teachers can become "store blind." They can get so close to the exam that they can't see the problems with it. It is much easier to correct a confusing question before the exam than deal with the impact of the confusion later during the test or when you are grading it. Don't assume your first attempt to make a test is perfect. In fact, it is wise to assume the opposite. Essay questions and matching, especially, are prone to problems. Be careful.

## Point 5: Make Objective Tests Easy to Grade

With just a little care, short-answer exams can be made much easier to grade. Before you give any exam, imagine how you will grade it. (Where will you sit? What will you do? What do you want to guard against?)

For example, in multiple choice, one way to guard against cheating is to ask students to circle the number or letter in the choices and put the number or letter in a space to the left. I have had some wiley students try to pass off an *a* as a *d*, or vice versa. Asking them to circle the answer will help eliminate any argument over whether the student wrote an *a* or a *d*. I work from the following principle: I don't believe students will cheat, but I don't lead them into temptation.

One way to make exams easier to grade is to always place the space for the number or letter to the left of the paper if you are right-handed and the staple in the top left. (If you are left-handed, you might find it easier to place the spaces on the right of the paper and the staple in the top right.) Don't believe that you must make exams just like those you have taken. Experiment with formats. You might discover something that works well for both you and your students.

## Point 6: Don't Use All the Same Sorts of Essay Questions

Take care to give different types of essay questions to students. Here are some samples for constructing essay test items of different types.

### Short Answer Fact-Based Questions

1.  Define the following musical terms:
    a.  half note
    b.  bass clef

### Inference Thought Questions

1.  Name one advantage and one disadvantage of the Walkman Personal Stereo System. Give an example for both the advantage and disadvantage.
2.  How has the automobile affected the way humans interact with each other? Give three examples.

### Remembering Facts

1.  Outline how technology has changed one of the primary industries in Canada.
2.  Give a short overview about how and when Canadian industrialization took place. As you answer this question, list five facts about industrialization.

3. Give two examples about how technology has had adverse effects on the food chain.

### Personal Opinion

1. Define change. In your definition make sure to give two examples of change.
2. Define progress. In your definition, make sure to give examples of progress. (Hint: You might want to show how your own definition of progress might differ from the definitions of other people.
3. What are three of the most important choices you will have to make in the future? For each choice you list, note why it is important to you.

## Point 7: Sometimes a Research Project Can Take the Place of a Test

Although I believe a final exam is important, it is not the only way to evaluate students. With some classes and some students, alternatives to final evaluations might be good choices. One alternative is a directed research project.

Should you choose the directed research project, here is a small sample of the kinds of research questions that would fit most texts and topics. Decide yourself how extensive the research question should be. Your directions to students should reflect this extensiveness.

1. Should the Canadian government censor sexist lyrics in music or music that calls for humans to respond violently to particular situations?
2. Research the agricultural practices of the Amish. (Would their ideas about using machines be an important consideration for Canadians?)
3. Hydroelectricity is electricity produced from water power. Although this process produces little pollution, the construction of dams to produce this water power has been controversial. Considering the environmental impact, both good and bad, is hydroelectricity a good source of energy?
4. What function does the ozone layer perform? Can the destruction of the ozone layer be stopped or delayed?

## Point 8: Dare to Be Different

The old poker saying goes: if you have a hunch, bet a bunch. Don't be afraid to try different things. It is surprising how often they work. Even if all your ideas don't work, as long as students aren't harmed by your choice, making a mistake in your classroom is not terrible.

One of my most successful "Wild Ideas" was to have students take a test in pairs of two. I had thought about doing it for a couple of years, but I anticipated that the lazier students would get even lazier if they were given the chance to depend on others; and no doubt this happens sometimes. But when I finally tried my idea, the real surprise was that none of the students wanted to be the weak link in the partnership. In my experience, the situation actually encouraged both partners to work harder in their preparation for the exam—just what I wanted to happen. Plus, I had only half the exams to grade. I did not, by the way, have trouble with noise during the short-answer, essay questions.

## Point 9: Don't Argue with Students in Class.

I believe it is always wise to review an exam in class. First, it gives you the chance to repeat and explain the content one more time. Second, it is possible that you made an error. I am very careful when I grade exams. I always add the marks twice. Still, I make errors. When we review an exam, I tell students that if I made an error in their favor they shouldn't tell me. However, if I made an error that causes them to lose points, they should tell me by writing me a note and returning it with their test paper. I will then check their note.

If they believe that I have graded an answer unfairly, I do not allow them to explain why in class. Rather, I ask them write me a note briefly explaining their case and justifying their position. I never allow them to argue a grading point in class. I do this for two reasons—the first is practical, the second pedagogical. First, I do not want the class to degenerate and ruin the tone I have been trying to establish. Second, I want to place the burden of proof on them. In effect, by stating their case and justifying their position they are gaining the very skills I wanted to teach them in the first place.

If they write me a note, I consider the case they make. Often I agree with them, but not always. Either way, I respond personally to the note they have written and if I agree, I add a mark to the grade book. (Note: teaching is as much an attitude as an action. With a little thought, even a mistake can turn into a teaching opportunity.)

## Point 10: Always Err on the Side of the Students

I make it a point to give the students the benefit of every doubt. If there is a case where I am sure I am correct, I don't give in. However, in cases where it's either one way or the other, I always give the point to the student. If you don't err on the side of the students, the reputation you gain might become detrimental to your relationship with them. Students simply don't respond well to teachers they believe are out to get them.

# HOW TO DO QUICK QUIZZES

You may wonder as you read this book: "Why is this person so enamored with evaluation?" So far, I have encouraged you to make huge, comprehensive exams, to review vocabulary and test it, to send tests home, and to evaluate whenever possible. Quite simply, my experience teaching at all levels has taught me the power of a variety and large number of evaluations.

Having many grades for a report card is also practical. One student assignment might vary widely; however, over a period of time a student's work will tend to gravitate toward the student's general ability. My own children have brought home report cards where their percentage grade had dropped from 83 to 65 in one report card period. When asked why, they say (and teachers confirm it) that the entire grade for the report card period was based on only one exam. What happens when a young person who is fighting the flu and is on medication that makes him or her drousy, takes an exam? Often when students say "it's not fair," they have a point. Having lots of grades will help eliminate these problems.

Let me review some of the benefits of exams.

1.  They let the students know where they are grade-wise.
2.  They encourage students to do their best.
3.  If students start to be successful on little things, I have found they gain more success on big things.
4.  Parents know where their kids are at (what they are studying and how they are doing).
5.  Students get to show off their good grades to their parents or others who care.
6.  Constant evaluation keeps the class on-task and gives your work focus.
7.  Constant evaluation helps students get better grades. When this happens, the class loses one of the reasons for conflict between teacher and students.
8.  The teacher and the students can work cooperatively to "beat the exam." The task becomes one of aiming for mutual goals; and when goals are accomplished, the team can take credit.
9.  It outlines the curriculum task. Once it is clear that the content to be covered has been covered, the class is more open for other enrichment activities.

10. A large number of evaluations allows the teacher to justify grades—especially the good ones—to school administrators.

11. Smaller quizzes can be placed in students' notebooks to help them study for larger, comprehensive exams which basically review the shorter quizzes. Frequent testing encourages students to learn organizational skills.

12. Because different students have different abilities (some have poor language skills), a large number and variety of different evaluations allow some students to succeed on one evaluation, even though they may find others more difficult. Often in a class with few evaluations, the odds are stacked against some students, no matter how hard they work, because they do not have the skills to succeed on a particular activity.

## The Concept of a Quick Quiz

When I use the term "quick quiz", I mean a short quiz of about 25 points that evaluates how well students know a smaller amount of material. The basic idea of a quick quiz is to test all the important material within a small section, not to be selective. (If there is to be selection, that might come in the comprehensive exam. However, my personal encouragement to teachers is to make their comprehensive exams really comprehensive. Test everything that is important.)

I encourage teachers to give quick quizzes (not necessarily pop quizzes) for every chapter they use in a textbook. I also encourage teachers to use a variety of different quick quizzes. You will notice that these activities are similar to the review activities presented throughout the rest of this book of ideas. The only real difference between the review activities and the quick quizzes is that the quick quizzes are done without an open book.

## A List of Possibilities

To help with ideas for quick quizzes, I offer you directions and a sample of different types of quick quizzes. The forms are easy enough to follow in making your own. Again, my encouragement is to save all the quizzes that you create for any curriculum unit. They will be helpful in the years to come, and for making trades with other teachers.

Remember that these are only samples of activities. The real quick quiz would have about 20-30 points.

### EXAMPLE ONE: MATCHING

*Directions:* Match the term or person on the left with the correct definition on the right. After you find the correct answer, mark the letter of the definition on the right in the space in front of the term on the left.

_____ 1. change
_____ 2. society
_____ 3. industrial process
a. the shifts, modifications, and new ways in which we do business, the businesses we have, and how we live our lives
b. a group of people with the same cultural patterns of living
c. how things are made by industry

## EXAMPLE TWO: TRUE OR FALSE

Directions: Read the following statements. If the statement is true, write true in the space to the left of the statement. If it is false, write false in the space. If the statement is false, tell why it is false.

_____ 1. Poetry is a literary genre made popular in the twentieth century.

_____ 2. The scientific definition of work is the force necessary to move an object over a distance.

_____ 3. Within the next fifty years, most Canadians will live to see the end of technology.

## EXAMPLE THREE: MULTIPLE CHOICE

Directions: Read the statements below. Underneath these statements are a number of choices. Pick the one that is most correct. When you have chosen this answer, circle it and write it in the space to the left of the number.

_____ 1. Technology
a. means the use of materials to accomplish tasks
b. is usually concerned with production
c. solves practical problems
d. all of the above
e. a and c only

_____ 2. The term that best describes a living organism that is able to manufacture its own food is
a. a plant
b. an animal
c. a human
d. protozoa

_____ 3. Technology began
a. with the production of the toothbrush
b. with the production of the laser disc
c. as soon as humans began to organize their labor
d. with the production of the computer

## EXAMPLE FOUR: MISSING WORDS

Directions: Below you will find sentences with words missing. Under these sentences, you will find a list of words that could complete the sentence. Only one word will correctly fit each blank. Pick the correct word or phrase from the list below and fill in the blank in the sentence above. Make sure your spelling is accurate.

1. A democracy works on the concept of the _____.
2. The term _____ refers to any decision making that promotes the best interests of the public.
3. _____ means the act of buying or using up goods.
4. The three levels of government are _____, _____, and _____.

    Choices: politics, rule of the majority, consumption, programs, copyright, local, politics, income, federal, provincial, local, jurisdiction.

## EXAMPLE FIVE: STRUCTURED ANSWER

Directions: Identify the following. In your answers provide information that would (1) suggest that you know what these parts of the human body do and (2) why these parts of the human body are important for the maintenance of human life).

1. bladder
2. esophagus
3. superior vena cave
4. pancreas
5. ribs

## EXAMPLE SIX: DEFINITIONS AND SENTENCES

Directions: Define the following terms. After each definition, write a sentence that uses the term you have defined in a real-life context. (Hint: It's not acceptable for this activity to write a sentence that is a redefinition of the term.)

1. saturated
2. chemical
3. anabolic steroid
4. biodegradable
5. leukemia

## EXAMPLE SEVEN: SYNTHESIS

Directions: The chapter you have just finished focuses on how technology can work to improve human life. In each of the following five areas, give one way that technology can improve life for Canadians.

1. the Great Lakes
2. forest management
3. farming
4. the environment
5. the future

*A Rule About Classroom Quizzes:* Do not ask the students to grade each other's quizzes in class. Except for spelling, there is no pedagogical justification for the practice. It's lazy. Students make mistakes. And it's an encouragement for cheating because friends will help friends. (Students may learn not to work but, instead, to lean on trickery to get by.) Last, having students grade each other's quizzes in class will generate the ire of thinking parents. It's a false economy. It may seem that having students grade their own quizzes or exams is saving you time, but the protracted hassle of dealing with one angry parent is not worth the minutes it saves. I encourage you as forcefully as I can: don't do it!

# HOW TO MAKE A GOOD FIRST IMPRESSION

The well-known shampoo television commercial says "There's only one chance to make a good first impression." On the first day of class, students watch their teachers carefully. Even if the teacher has a well-worn reputation, whether good or bad, they watch.

When you meet your classes for the first time, they will be sizing you up and building an evaluation that they will use all year long. Just in the past week, I've heard junior high students I know use these nicknames for their teachers: "the PMS Queen" and "Mr. Get Downwind."

Students are like the rest of us. We all tend to make snap judgments about people, based on first impressions. It might not be right, but it's what we do. You can help your own cause by making a good first impression. You can harm your cause if you don't.

Here are some ways a teacher can make a good first impression.

## 1. Dress Neatly and Appropriately

The first thing people see is your outside appearance. To be neat and appropriately dressed does not mean that you must have an expensive wardrobe. Quite the contrary. My experience is that people who get in a fashion contest with students (especially at the high school level) detract from their teaching.

But clothes make a statement. I think it is important to set yourself apart from your students. Some people suggest that you should give your students the idea you are approachable and "one of them" by the way you dress. My experience suggests that doesn't work as well. Your dress is an important factor (because it's a low-force method of control—much like expecting to be called Mrs., Mr., or Miss) in helping you set a classroom structure. If you can distance yourself without force, you can create a more comfortable structure for your students. Here's an axiom: all humans are more comfortable with structure than they are without it. The corollary to the axiom is that structure should be liberating, not debilitating.

## 2. Arrive on Time

Coming to class on time is another low-force way to set a comfortable structure. Without saying a word, students know that you care about what you do and are serious about your job. We all, especially young people, appreciate people who care to do well, especially when their doing well concerns us.

If you watch teachers for long, you'll soon notice that many of the students' favorite teachers meet and welcome their students at the door of the classroom. There's a lesson here. One high school teacher I know shakes hands with every student who comes into his class each day. It may sound silly, but it makes a visible difference in how his class is run. It works for him.

On time means always being on time. Here's a hint: always start your class right on time and end when the period is over. My experience is that when I quit giving free time in my class, to "work on homework or other assignments," I cut discipline problems in half. If you get into a time-carving mode, where you carve a minute off the front end of class and leave a minute free at the back end of class, it becomes like leveling table legs. The process never seems to stop. Soon you'll be teaching 12 minutes out of a 50-minute class. Because your classroom is run so inefficiently, you must make up for it by giving lots of homework—just to keep up. You'll soon get the reputation of being a "slave-driver." You can't win at this game.

## 3. Smell Good

Smelling good probably goes without saying, or does it? Unfortunately, sometimes teachers don't smell good and this can detract from every other aspect of their teaching. Odor includes both odor of the body and breath odor. Some perfumes and colognes are overpowering and should be avoided too. Here's the rule: never let things other than teaching distract from teaching.

## 4. Use Good Posture and Positioning

Body language is the steam that indicates the boil within. We can know, or at least think we can know, a lot about people from how they carry themselves. Consider how and where you stand or sit in the classroom. If you need to, arrange your classroom to enhance the position (in both senses of the word) you wish to take. A rigid goose-stepping teacher will convince students of one thing; a slouch will convince them of another.

Watch yourself teach and try to eliminate mannerisms that distract from what you want to do. If you have an unavoidable mannerism (like stuttering) have the sense to turn it into a positive thing. Teaching is about building relationships. Despite their bad reputation, students are the most straightforward, loving, and protective people—when they like the teacher. They can accept almost anything. The big plus in your relationship with students is that if students know you care about them and want to help them, they will accept almost anything you do. You'll be surprised how many students have a parenting instinct; if they like you, they will protect you from others.

## 5. Use Eye Contact and Facial Expression

When students get close enough to look at you, it's the eyes and the face they look at first. Eye contact that takes place on the first day of class can set the tone for the rest of the year. It can be used to show anger, fear, confusion, impending conflict, and can convince students to expect a war. Or it can show confidence, concern, celebration, approachableness, and hint at the promise of a good class and a great year together. You can also tell a lot about your students by how they look at you.

Here's a simple hint: glance at students. If there is eye contact, smile. Don't do it to the same people all the time, but make sure that by the end of the first week you have tried to made a "contact contract" with each of your students.

## 6. Be Approachable

One of the keys to successful teaching is, I think, to be both different and the same. There must be some distance between the teacher and the students, quite simply because there are times when someone has to control the classroom and that someone MUST be you—the teacher. Don't confuse approachable behavior for adolescent behavior. You are not their peer, but their teacher.

When you interact with your students, be polite and personal. You might have heard the same stories of woe over and over, but they are probably very important for that student. If you want to let them know you care, simply learn their names quickly and use them. Research suggests that kids like it whenever people know their names. I try to follow this rule: when you are there, be there. This means don't be the kind of person who, while talking with students, pays attention to everything else going on around—continually glancing here and there and showing them that you would rather be elsewhere.

## 7. Do Not Be Condescending

My theory is that condescending people are unhappy people, trying hard to get happier. First, they equate power with happiness, and they believe that they don't have enough power. So they attempt to get happy by grabbing all the power they can. Second, they wrongly believe that there is a finite amount of happiness in the world and that happiness can be balanced by taxing it progressively. They attempt to get happier by making the people around them unhappy.

Another problem with condescending people is that they know it all. They never listen to things all the way through and have answers to questions that have not yet been asked. The problem is not that they lack knowledge, but that they attempt to lord their knowledge over others. Think about what you think about. If you get your thoughts straight on the inside, you cannot possibly be condescending on the outside.

## Remember the concept of CHEAP talk
## (Use a <u>C</u>onfident, <u>H</u>elpful, <u>E</u>ager, <u>A</u>udible, <u>P</u>leasant Voice)

Confidence and nervousness are not the same thing. Most good and experienced teachers still get nervous. Teaching carries a responsibility. Still, you can be confident about what you can be confident about. If you are well-planned for unit one, you can probably be confident about your first week. Your voice and what you say can show that you are excited about being where you are.

There is a difference in the reaction of people to a prophet of doom and gloom and the bringer of good news. Alexander the Great was so enamored by positive thinking that he executed any messenger who brought bad news. Here's another hint: if you have good news, say it right away; swallow twice before you bring bad news.

## 9. Look and Be Well-Organized

It is difficult for young teachers to be well-organized about their whole year. But, there is no excuse for not organizing something during the first year. And every year there is time to organize something new. Here are three hints:

- What you plan, plan well. It is ultimately more fruitful to plan one unit completely and all the way through than to plan two units only partly.
- Systematically save what you do from one year to the next.
- Find a like-minded co-worker who will share the task. You'll cut your work in half.

One way to look well-organized is to prepare and tell a story from your subject area. No matter what your subject, there is a story you can prepare and tell. You have three purposes in telling the story: providing information, making your subject area interesting, and supporting the thesis that this teacher "really knows his or her stuff." When you tell your story, provide names and personalities to the characters, human emotions, and human dilemma. Learn the story inside out and practice telling it well. Every year prepare one new story and be ready to tell it. Sometime during the year, you will feel the need to "get off topic" with your story. Your students will love it. This story can often be referred to throughout the year.

## 10. Use Humor, Up to a Point

What do kids really want from their teachers? My experience tells me that you only have to give them two things to keep them satisfied:

- They want to be treated fairly.
- They don't want to be bored.

## WHAT WORKS

Why use humor? Because humor is an invitation to enjoyment. Here's a rule: become more serious about helping students learn content, but bring humor to how you teach that content.

If there's a choice between having fun and not having fun, always choose fun. If there's a choice between being active and not being active, always choose activity. And always, work from a theory of success.

# HOW TO TEACH PEACEFULLY

Until recently, most people believed that peace education was about how many nuclear bombs will blow up major US or Soviet cities, how far away a person must live from an explosion to survive the initial blast, or how to protest against the cruise missile. But peace education is much more than a subject area with a content that centers on war and mayhem. Peace education should be an everyday activity for the teacher. Peace education is broader than simply a study of war; in fact, its content centers on how to live and interact with people, especially people within a classroom.

The purpose of peace education (teaching peacefully) is nothing less than building the kind of world that most of us want to live in and educating the kind of people most of us want in that world. Does this sound like pie-in-the-sky? The fact that it sounds naive to many people points out one of the weaknesses of our educational system.

I do not find the position neutrality to be useful. In the name of neutral teaching and of "not pushing our own philosophies on students," teachers have been afraid to point out problems in the human interactions in the school. We have neglected to break down structural patterns that enslave us. We have accepted rudeness and boorish behavior as the norm, letting it go by without comment. As a result, I believe, many people have been hurt.

Don't confuse my rhetoric about teaching peacefully with libertarianism on one hand or ultra-conversatism on the other. Instead, consider what you believe about how people should be treated. Then remember the important vocation of a teacher. Without daring to risk conflict, without daring to take a strong stand either for or against, and without daring to state what you believe, there is every chance that positive human relationships in the classroom will disintegrate.

If you want to teach peacefully, to encourage peace education in the one-on-one interactions of classroom life, and to work towards the vital education of young people who can and will take responsibility for creating and shaping positive human interactions, let me make some suggestions about how you should live in the classroom. First, there are some things you should not do and you probably already know what they are. Don't do these things. Second, there are some things you should do. Again, you can probably make a quick list. And again, my advice is simple. Do them. Implementing these good things can be a more difficult task, but it is one worth pursuing.

## What Not to Do

1.  Avoid pitting students against each other. Restrict extreme competition, the kind of competition where people are psychologically hurt. The competition of gaming activities gets the blood flowing and can serve as an educational encouragement, but it is very easy to cross the line. It is also very easy to know when the line has been crossed. Don't base your classroom activity on competition.

2.  Don't put students down. Eliminate all classroom ridicule of people and opinions. As soon as one student criticizes another person in a way that is rude, stop it. An attitude of tolerance does not include rude and destructive behavior. A certain amount of idea conflict is required for learning to take place, but I have seen teachers actively encourage painful conflict in the name of academic debate. Not only have the results been painful for someone, but the whole experience has produced more heat than light. It just wasn't worth it.

3.  Avoid power-seeking. Some teachers are in love with the position of teaching because it puts them in front of and in charge of others. They forget that teaching is more service to than service from. If you are to teach peacefully, you cannot try to preach or seek power. Do not view your students as the enemy. If there is to be any conflict, the conflict metaphor should be one of you and the students together as a team against a difficult curriculum. Don't set yourself up as the "Perfect" Teacher. If you do, you will fail.

    For example, watch how you write comments on students' papers. It's just as easy to say "I'm confused. Remember that you're writing for someone else to understand, in this case, a simple-minded teacher." as it is to write "Your sentence structure is very poor. Your writing doesn't make any sense." In both cases, you get the same point across. But in the first instance you don't take the chance of abusing the student. You also subtly point to the need of the writer to consider the audience.

    In addition, a bit of self-deprecation is a very acceptable and long-standing form of classroom humor. As I repeated earlier in the book, it also shows that a person can make a mistake without terrible consequences. I am a kind of sloppy, non-stylish, run-of-the mill university professor. In my classroom, my lack of style and fashion soon become cause for a mild form of humor, and students often joke that "You can take him out, but you can't dress him up." Humor helps build relationships.

4.  Don't focus on one side of a dispute. It is hard not to have favorites in your classroom, but don't let personal feelings get in the way of hearing what's happening. Listen. Don't be inflexible.

5. Don't make stereotypical statements. Don't reveal your prejudices about people. If you have prejudices or believe in stereotypes, think about why you do so. You may have to change yourself. Even if you do continue to believe that your prejudices and stereotypes are true, you can not use the class as a forum to preach them.

## What to Do

1. Stress compromise.
2. Consider the needs of the individual.
3. Stress personal achievement.
4. Use positive reinforcement.
5. Treat students fairly.
6. Ensure equal rights for students. This might not mean equal action; instead, it might mean the right to treat students differently, based on your best knowledge about individual differences. For example, it would simply be unfair to require a student who, for lack of funds, does not have access to magazines for an assignment. It would be acting differently, but "fairly," to provide magazines for one student but not provide them for another.
7. Stress tolerance. Everyone should have a say in the functioning of the classroom. Listen, then decide. Work to reduce the superiority attitude that can creep into a classroom situation. This includes the superiority attitude of those "good" students for whom school seems to be built; and it also might include your own superior attitude.
8. Work to improve communication within class discussion. Especially strive to promote work through projects and group work.
9. Create decision-making bodies within the classroom to solve conflicts. You can't know all of what's going on (your students' views), but you can work to try to know what's going on.
10. Stress building and understanding the concept of positive power. Positive power is the power to do good. It is not the same as negative power, which manipulates and enslaves.
11. Promote multiculturalism (active tolerance). This tolerance is not just a national goal; it's a personal goal. Remember that we all have differences. If you learn to love teaching, my guess is that one thing you love are the unique differences among your students. Don't focus on "negative differences." Students in your classroom fear not measuring up. They are very aware of their differences and are extremely sensitive about how they "don't fit in." One of your jobs as a teacher is to accept and encourage your students, differences and all. Remember, it's the differences that make students so much fun.

12. Promote learning about others. One way to do this is to begin by actively thinking about the fundamental basis of conflict and "tribalism." This activity will broaden students perspectives, as well as your own.

13. Let opinions stay opinions. Students' opinions are not things to be swayed or personal challenges for the teacher to overcome. Remember, people always have opinions. Draw a line between what should be challenged and what doesn't really matter. My rule is that opinions and statements should be challenged if they cause someone to suffer or if they hinder you from doing your best job as a teacher.

14. Expect your class to be managed and your students to be self-disciplined. You are the teacher; you manage your own classroom. Eventually, you must expect your students to manage their own behavior. If you don't expect it, they never will. Remember, and this is one of the most important lessons a teacher can learn, discipline is a positive structure rather than a negative chain.

15. Admit mistakes when you make them. Everyone has the right to make an honest mistake. Mistakes are not always enjoyable, but there is a positive side to making a mistake. You can learn from it. Education is, in part, the ability to change behavior. The attitude that we all make honest mistakes and can move beyond them, creates an atmosphere for positive risk-taking. The students are watching, both when you do well and when you do not. They are especially interested in how your react to your own mistakes. From your reactions, they will learn how they should react.

16. Work from a metaphor of respect. Good teachers have rules for living in their classrooms. Some are verbal and are expressed with the phrase: "These are things we won't do." Some are silent principles for living. One of the best of these silent principles is to do nice things for people in and out of class.

17. Provide a positive atmosphere.

18. Become self-aware and honest. Acknowledge both your strengths and your weaknesses. Admit your strengths. (It is often easier to admit weaknesses than strengths.) You probably don't have all the talents, but you do have some. Use what you have. This will make you happy. And when you are happy, your students will be happy.

19. Work at the students' level. If you don't, you will frustrate them. It seems simple, but when people are frustrated, they respond in frustration.

20. Remember what you are there for. You are a teacher. Do the job.

# PART II
## Ideas for Teaching

# HOW TO HELP STUDENTS REVIEW
# HOW A TEXTBOOK IS WRITTEN

Here are two facts about textbooks: (1) there are many textbooks and (2) textbooks are written by real people and published by real publishing houses, with real and different ideas about what is important and what makes them attractive. Sometimes teachers forget that students are especially naive about what happens in school. (I was about 13 before I found out that teachers did not live at school.) If we act in a way that assumes students understand how textbooks are organized, we presume a great deal. Often we are wrong.

Since textbooks are so widely used as education tools, it would seem that a lesson about how a textbook is put together would benefit students. Yet, I have never seen another teacher use an activity that looks at how textbooks are organized. The activity below may help. It is a general idea that helps students explore parts of the textbook. It is relatively painless, and when students get finished, they should know at least something about the sections of the book you are using.

This activity is created as an example, but the style can be adapted to any text by changing the specific questions. [Note: You might want to consider using this activity with the next one on Scavenger Hunts.]

## Example of a Text Worksheet

1. The Table of Contents
   a. How many sections are there in Chapter 3?
   b. How many chapters are there in the book?
   c. How many Case Studies are there in Chapter 6? What are their titles?
   d. The end of each chapter is very similar. What four features are contained in each chapter?
   e. On what page would you find information about safety rules in science classrooms?
2. The Chapters
   a. What symbol is found on the first page of each chapter? What do you think this symbol tells you about the book?

      b. In each chapter there are several "blocked off" sections. What types of information do you find "blocked off" in these sections.

      c. What do you find on the bottom of many pages in the text?

3. The Glossary

      a. What is the definition of integer?

      b. How many words are defined that begin with the letter L? What are they?

      c. What is the difference between a square and a rhombus?

4. The Index

      a. What is the first entry listed under the letter M?

      b. On what page would you find information about cloud formations?

      c. How many times in the textbook is electricity talked about?

# HOW TO DO A SCAVENGER HUNT

The textbook is, and will probably continue to be, the most widely used resource in any subject area. Yet many teachers don't use the textbook in a systematic and rigorous way. We may do a pretty good job helping our students learn the content, but there are a variety of other skills we can help students learn in addition to learning the content.

The following ideas were compiled for two reasons. First, I think teaching should be more enjoyable. Second, I believe that students can and should learn important study and academic skills while they are learning content.

## Brief Overview: The Scavenger Hunt

A scavenger hunt is a game where people hunt for and try to collect a variety of objects or pieces of information. The person or team who collects the most pieces wins the game. With a little adaptation of this basic idea, such a game can be converted into a useful teaching idea.

My purpose is simple. I want to help my students know how a book is put together, what parts are in a book, and how authors think about what's important. To accomplish this goal, I use scavenger hunts to send students around the book instead of around the neighborhood. During their trip, they will be introduced to things like the Table of Contents, the Glossary, the Index, the Chapters, and so on. The activity accomplishes the same objectives as the previous activity, but changes the form. This activity is more like a game. The previous activity is more like a worksheet. As they complete the scavenger hunt, students will also get an opportunity to see how pictures work in relationship to text, how questions are written, and how chapters are laid out.

Instead of telling students how a book is put together, teachers provide opportunities that allow students to learn by themselves. At the same time, students have some fun as they learn. By the time they have finished the process, students will know more about the book than they did when they started. They may even have enjoyed the activity.

I encourage this Scavenger Hunt as a beginning exercise, although teachers could save it for "one of those days" when they just need to get through the day, go home, and go to bed. The directions should be brief but clear so that students do not have any difficulty with them. The ideas could be used in small group competitions or as individual activities. Every choice has a trade-off. The trade-off here is that individual activities are the most educational, but group competitions are the most fun.

I would encourage this as an in-class activity. However, if you like to give homework, the assignment can be given as homework. As a third step, and a way to gather some insight into how the students are doing, you might give students the opportunity to make up a small scavenger hunt for themselves or for the class. When this activity is completed, I would encourage a wrap-up of about 5-10 minutes that reviews with students what they have learned.

There are many variations of the main scavenger-hunt theme. The two examples I will give here are (1) Scavenger Math and (2) Scavenger Sleuth.

## Scavenger Math Problems

Again, these examples are based on a ficticious textbook, but can be adapted to any text.

### Problem #1

**Directions**

This Scavenger Math problem is an adding problem. Read each of the parts of the problem. When you find the correct answer, place it in the space in the sentence. Then write it on a separate line, just like you are making a math problem. Add each of the numbers as you go, but when you are finished, check your work. It's the student with the right answer who wins, not the first one done.

1.  An index can help you if you want to look up a particular topic. Find the first page of the Index. Wait a minute, it doesn't have a page number. If it did, that page number would be _____.

2.  Find the Table of Contents (called Contents in this book). It tells you the chapter titles and the subtitles within the chapter. There are three questions about this Table of Contents for you.
    a. How many chapters are there in this book? _____
    b. Which chapter number has six subheadings? _____
    c. In which chapter would you find a discussion about flowers? _____

3.  Chapter One talks about China's geography. How many maps are there in this chapter? _____

    *Answer:* You should have found five numbers in these three questions. Add them up. Your answer is _____.

*Problem #2*

**Directions**

This Scavenger Math problem is a subtraction problem. Read each of the parts of the problem. When you find the correct answer, place it in the space in the sentence. Then write it on a separate line, just like you are making a math problem. Subtract each number as you go, and when you are finished check your work. Remember, it's the student with the right answer who wins, not the first one done.

1. The Glossary gives you a list of important words used in the book and their definitions. The last page of the Glossary in this book is page _____.

2. There are lots of parts of a book that give information, but certainly not for your learning about science. Page ii gives information to help libraries who want to catalogue the book for their shelves. It also gives information about the author. This one shows that the author is still alive and in what year he was born. If the author was born on January 13th, how old is he or she? _____.

3. In this book, important words that students might not know are defined on the bottom of pages where they are found. Chapter 12 is a short chapter, but it has lots of important words. How many vocabulary words are found on the bottom of the pages in Chapter 12?

_____

*Answer:* You should have found three numbers in these three questions. Subtract the number you found in 2 from the number you found in 1. Then subtract the number you found in 3. What is your final answer?

## Scavenger Sleuth Problem

**Directions**: Scavenger Sleuth is a word game. The goal is to complete an important sentence about Japan using the clues given. When you find the missing words for each question, write them down on a piece of paper. Once you have all the words, put them in the right order to make the sentence. This sentence will give you an important bit of information about Iceland. The first person or team to complete the sentence correctly is the winner.

1. Two words are found four times in the chapter titles of this book (not counting 'is'). They are _____ and _____. Write the longest word on your sheet of paper.

2. On pages 75 and 167 of the book, there are two pictures. In each picture, the person shown on the left is (older, younger) than the people on the right in the picture. Write the correct word on your sheet of paper.

3. In Chapter 7, three subheadings start with the same word. Write this word on your piece of paper.

4. Every chapter has three sets of questions at the end. What is the first word in the titles of these questions? Write it on your sheet of paper.

5. Pictures in the book show what life in Iceland is like. Read the caption on page 94. Write the third word of the second sentence on your sheet of paper.

6. The map on page 4 of the book shows the distribution of _____. Write this word on your paper.

Look at these words you have written. Arrange them in a sentence that reveals an important fact about Iceland. What is this fact?

# HOW TO GIVE STUDENTS NOTES

Giving students notes is one of the most important teaching techniques. It presumes that there is a body of knowledge that students ought to learn and that the teacher (or some other authority) has the responsibility to order and synthesize this knowledge in a systematic fashion. These presuppositions are quite accurate.

Learning how to judge important information for note-taking is a skill that students learn in elementary and junior high school and practice throughout the remainder of their academic careers. Sometimes, students should choose their own notes. At other times, the teacher should choose the material that students should attend to. Giving notes is more than sorting and dishing out. There are many ways that teachers can choose to "dish out" the information.

Over and over again, I hear the statement that students get bored with lectures. There is more than some truth to the statement. But in their attempts to make every activity exciting, teachers sometimes throw out the baby with the bath water. They respond by refusing to provide information (through lecture or notes) to their students. They forget about content in the name of process. Without content, teachers find teaching almost impossible.

Variety is always a key to successful teaching. If teachers want to choose from the variety of options, it helps if they know the options. The list that follows offers a summary of 40 ways that teachers can give notes. Not all of them are exciting for all the students all the time. But each is a legitimate teaching activity—useful some of the time. My theory is that most students will tolerate any activity, even if it is deadly boring, if they can see a reason for doing the activity and if the activity is used sparingly.

My hint to individual teachers is this: while you are looking at the list, cross out those that you believe are either too dull, too difficult to understand, or redundant. Second, add to the list ideas that are your own.

1.  **Group Discussion:** Split the class into working groups of four people. Split the material to be covered into sections of equal length, one for each group. Have each group take responsibility for one of the sections, asking them to give eight to ten points from their reading that the rest of the class should know. Have them give group reports or make visuals.

2.  **Lecture:** This is the tried and true method. Without writing on the

board, highlight the section to be studied orally to your students, directing them to take notes about the most important sections. Ten minutes before the class is over, review and evaluate orally what students took as notes.

3.  **Overhead:** Write notes on the overhead for students to copy. Direct students to write these notes into their notebook as they are written on the overhead. As students are copying these notes verbatim, embellish the notes with additional comments.

4.  **Blackboard:** Write your notes on the blackboard and ask students to copy them directly into their notebooks. When they have finished copying these notes, discuss them with the students, embellishing them with extra ideas.

5.  **The Two Hat Technique:** In sections where there are different points of view or perspectives that could be brought out (i.e., different sides during a war, strike, or conflict, or how different social classes or ethnic groups might see an incident in history), use two different hats as props. As you are discussing one side of the issue, put the hat representing that side on. As you switch to the other side, change hats. This technique will work well when the teacher is quite familiar with both sides or perspectives of an issue.

6.  **Student Responsibilities:** Give students responsibilities for taking their own notes by studying the material to be covered on their own and producing one of the following products:
    *   a transparency to be used by the teacher
    *   a storyboard or cartoon depicting an event or historical incident
    *   a rap music song
    *   a lesson plan that they can give the class by "being the teacher" for a moment
    *   a readers' theater, where groups of students sit on stools and read sections of text they have chosen as important
    *   a video for the class (i.e., a newscast, a panel, or a talk show)
    *   an oral or written story based on the event studied
    *   a puppet show

7.  **Posters:** Where appropriate, students can design posters based on the material to be covered (i.e., a travel poster for a geographical area studied, an election poster for a current or historical election, or a protest poster that highlights some world event).

8.  **Big Sheets of Recycled Paper:** Teachers can put their notes on large sheets of paper that can be hung in the room. Without taking class time, students can copy these notes during lag times in the class or when they have finished their other work.

9. **The Duplicate Copy:** Teachers can duplicate a copy of their own notes, past tests, and current test ideas. This can be made available on a checkout basis for students to take home. They can copy anything in the teacher's notes—even copies of the old tests.

10. **Worksheets:** Teachers can embed their notes with a variety of fill-in-the-blank worksheets or readings with questions and answers. By doing the worksheets, the students are taking the notes.

11. **Games and Puzzles:** Teachers can make word games out of the vocabulary notes. Some of these include crossword puzzles, hidden word searches, and sentences where the important word is jumbled with mixed-up letters.

12. **Demonstrations:** Teachers can demonstrate the notes in a dramatic fashion (or can have students playact the notes). Historical events, like the signing of peace treaties, strikes, or even battles can be described and enriched in an active manner.

13. **Storytelling:** Teachers can learn historical events so well that they can almost fictionalize them by a third-person omniscient viewpoint. It is intriguing to place feelings and emotions on the characters.

14. **Outline:** Teachers can provide the notes in an outline where main headings are separated from subheadings in a proper outline form.

15. **Screwed-up Outline:** Teachers can provide the skeleton of the outline (the numbers and letters). Underneath this outline skeleton, the teacher will place the sentences or phrases that should be placed in the skeleton. The student's job is to put the proper phrase in the proper spot in the framework.

16. **Pictures or Photos:** In a variation of storytelling, teachers could use photos or pictures of important aspects of the material as props and tell the story from the pictures (i.e., pictures of historical events or of people).

17. **Computer Programs:** Teachers who are adept or who have friends who are adept at computer programming can place a variety of notes into a computer program of "skill and drill" notetaking.

18. **Learning Stations/Modules:** Teachers can create a number of stations where students can listen, view, or copy notes. Students can then move from one station to another during a class period.

19. **Student Matching:** Teachers can place vocabulary words on one card and definitions on another. Create enough words and definitions so that every class member has either a word or definition. Pass them out to students. Have students find their match by moving around and talking to other students. When they have found their match, they should write down their word and their definition. They should then find others who have also matched and write down their vocab-

ulary terms and definitions. Do this until all students have all the terms. Review each of the pairs of terms and definitions. This activity can be repeated several times with the same terms.

20. **Class Debates:** Teachers can set up debates where students are split into two groups. Each group is given all the points to their side of the issue but not the points from the other. Students do not find their own information, but use only the material given by the teacher.

21. **"This Is/Was Your Life":** Students can set up a television show based on "This Is Your Life." The personality (or "thing") sits in center stage. From off-stage a voice gives information about relationships or events. Other characters then walk on stage to meet the character.

22. **Field trips:** Teachers can set up field trips to different places and take notes on what they find there. They can also set up a field trip scavenger hunt where students must go to different places around the school to find notes or the answers to questions from worksheets.

23. **Progressive Stuffer:** Students must go to different teachers (or other school personnel) to find hidden clues about a person or event in history. (One nice thing about this activity is that the student can meet people not normally seen as part of the school, but who are important. For example, the two most important people in any school are the school secretary and the janitor.)

24. **Treasure Hunt:** Notes can be hidden at different places around the school, and students must follow a treasure map to find them. (Students can set up this activity.)

25. **Archaeological Displays:** Teachers can bring in artifacts that highlight different pieces of information being studied and tell about these displays.

26. **Documentary Films:** Teachers can show films about historical incidents and use note-taking questions.

27. **Time Machine:** Teachers can take imaginary trips back through time and have students visualize events that are taking place.

28. **Webbing:** Using a web outline, with the major point in a circle at the middle and lines drawn to subpoints in circles around the major point, teachers can help students outline whole sections of text.

29. **Mindstorming:** After a section of the text is read by the class, teachers can have students try to remember the whole text by "mindstorming" (brainstorming) what they remember and using other people's memories to stir their own.

30. **Retrieval Charts:** Teachers can provide completed charts for students to use to retrieve information. These charts can also be left empty for students to fill in.

31. **Songs and Rhyme:** Teachers can create (or have students create) songs or rhymes with the notes in them. (Note: A teacher who plays the guitar and can compose a few simple songs will be a wonderful addition)

32. **Community Resource People:** Inviting people into class to tell about different time periods, geography, or historical incidents provides information to students. (It's always best to have students prepare questions to ask the visitors.)

33. **Create an Index:** Students can be directed to create an index for material they are reading. In the process of creating the index, they are choosing the most important material.

34. **Summary Paragraphs:** Have students read a section of text and write a four-sentence summary paragraph of the text.

35. **Dictate Notes:** Teachers can orally dictate notes that students copy verbatim. (Note: It's best to use this only for short periods of time.)

36. **True or False Audio Tape:** Students listen to the teacher or someone else give notes from a tape. They are given a set of notes with some accurate statements and some inaccurate statements. They are directed to write true or false beside the statement on the sheet as they listen to the tape.

37. **Student Question Market:** Ask students to read a section of text and write one or more questions and answers from that section. They set up a market where they trade questions with each other.

38. **Visual Association:** As the teacher reads a part of the text (or students can read their own text), they are directed to draw a picture that represents (or helps them visualize) that part of the text.

39. **Team Questions:** Split the class into two teams. Ask each team to review a chapter in 15 minutes and write questions for the other team. Take turns asking the other team these questions. If they can answer, they get 5 points. If they miss, they get none. This can be open book or closed book.

40. **Bulletin Board Answers:** Each day before class starts, place a question on the bulletin board that will be on the test. When class starts, the question comes down. (This also helps students get to class on time.)

*Hints:*

1. Once you have made an activity, carefully save it from year to year.

2. If students make good activities, ask for their permission to use them with future classes. (It saves you work and is positive reinforcement.)

3. Don't hesitate to choose a large number of student questions for your exams. Go over the ones you choose before you give the test. Show why these are good questions. You will be teaching both content and how to study and answer questions.

# HOW TO GET STUDENTS TO READ AND DISCUSS

Reading and discussing what you have read is a fundamental task for any classroom. To learn information that is not previously known, students must read it or hear it presented. To understand material that has some depth and breadth, students must often discuss it with others. Knowing that reading and discussion of the reading is so important to any classroom begs the question: How can we help students read and discuss the material that we want them to read and discuss?

Many of us have sat in classrooms where teachers have used one method exclusively. Often oral reading predominates the classroom activity. However, other methods like reading silently and then answering questions or working on worksheets are also commonly used. There is nothing pedagogically wrong with these ideas, if they are used properly and with a thoughtful perspective about what classroom goals should be. It's too bad that these activities are not always used thoughtfully. Like any method, even the most considered course of action can become boring if it is used too much.

When using any readings, there are a small number of central, common-sense learning principles that should not be ignored. Teaching experience and the body of research agree on some of these. Here's a short list:

1. Give students a purpose for reading. If students know why they are reading, they will be better able to focus their attention on the task.

2. Provide a directed reading activity (DRA) that will help focus their reading. A project (something to do), even a small one, helps students focus.

3. Get students off to a flying start. For example, a teacher who begins by reading the first paragraph with fluency and emotion helps make the rest of the reading easier for the students.

4. Look for and eliminate barriers to understanding before reading begins. For example, if there is vocabulary in a reading that most students will not know, it's just smart to help them learn it before reading. Students, particularly those with difficulty, might come to one word they don't understand, throw up their hands, and quit.

5. Provide bite-size chunks. Reading, like other activities, is best done in moderation. It is always best to quit before a task becomes boring.

## Ways to Read and Discuss

The following list of activities is provided to help teachers consider alternatives to oral reading or silent reading-answering questions. Without ignoring the real advantages of reading and discussion, the list attempts to answer the question: what are some of the many ways teachers can help students read and discuss material?

1. If the reading is about people, ask students to note the characteristics or actions of one of the characters. When the reading assignment is finished, ask them to portray one aspect of the character's personality or an action the character did.

2. Ask students to make quiz questions from the reading. If it is for an objective exam, ask them to create about five questions. If it is for a short answer exam, ask them to create two questions. They may trade these questions with classmates. (Note: Teachers should consider using these questions for their own exams.)

3. Ask students to create worksheets that would help others "get through" or get information from the reading.

4. Have students read orally and
   • provide teacher commentary at various times throughout the reading
   • put different students in charge of providing review/summary/commentary at various times throughout the reading

5. If the reading is photocopied, provide directions so that the students can color-code various sections. For example, if you are reading social studies, with a red pencil underline the German position during World War I. With a green pencil, underline the Allied position during World War I.

6. Play 'stump the teacher.' The student's task is to read a section of material and come up with the most difficult questions they can think of. Students then ask the questions they have designed, hoping to stump the teacher.

7. Use student questions as a starting point for discussion. As students are reading, ask them to write two discussion questions on a piece of scrap paper. Collect these questions and, as a leader, use them to direct discussion.

8. Focus on feelings. As students are reading, ask them to pick a person or group of people and try to imagine (and jot down) their feelings as they are reading the material. After the material is read, ask various students to share the people and their feelings. (For example, if your class is reading a novel set in the period of the Industrial Revolution like *Oliver Twist*, what were the feelings of the large factory owners, or the feelings of the workers who moved from the small farms to the factories, or the feelings of the families of both groups?)

9. Prepare for a short debate. Should the reading make it possible, provide a debate topic prior to reading. Split the class into two groups, representing different sides of the topic, and ask each group to read the section for support for their side of the debate. (For example, in science, should the government of Canada shut down all industries that cause harm to the environment?)

10. Design a short open-book quiz that students take as they are reading the assignment. This may be done individually or in groups of two students.

11. Make a worksheet of questions that students must answer as they read the text. These worksheets might be fill-in-the-blank or short answer.

12. Like a worksheet, make a puzzle that students can solve as they proceed through the reading. One type of puzzle uses sentences directly from the book with important words purposely left out. The puzzle asks students to find the sentence, putting the correct word into the space and using one of the letters in that work as a piece of a hidden message about the reading.

13. As they are reading, ask students to create a drawing (or cartoon) that illustrates an important point from the reading. These drawings can then be shared with other classmates in a large or small group.

14. Use a buddy system for small-group oral reading. In this system the buddies take turns orally reading the text. After, or during, their reading they can decide on the most important points from the reading to put into their notebooks.

15. Using a short piece of text, give students a piece of overhead projector film and ask them to prepare a sheet to go on the overhead projector. During the remainder of class, ask a number of these students to act like the teacher and come to the overhead and share their notes.

16. Using a buddy system, split a text into two equal parts. Give each buddy responsibility for reading one of the sections, preparing notes from that section, and teaching that section to the other buddy. After they have finished, give a short quiz to both students, averaging their grades.

17. If there are people (or countries) with different points of view involved in the reading, split the class into equal groups representing these different people, countries or points of view. Ask students to read the text with each group taking a particular perspective. After the reading is completed, split the room into "coffee table groups" where each person in the group discusses an issue in question from the particular perspective of the person, country, or point of view each has been given.

18. Play a true-or-false game with the students. After students have read the text, review the reading by making a number of important statements that come directly from the text—some of them accurate—some not accurate. Have students tell you whether the statement you make is accurate or not accurate. If it is not accurate, ask them to tell you why.

19. Play the same true-or-false game with the students as described in #18. But instead of waiting for students to read the material, play the game with texts open and the material in view. Their task then becomes to see how quickly they can find whether the statement you make is accurate or not accurate. (Note: Since one of the skills focused on in this option is learning how texts are written, as they are playing the game, you can help them with hints about how to find the material they are looking for.)

20. Help students focus on the vocabulary of the reading by making up a crossword sheet they can fill out as they are reading the textual material.

21. Help students learn the skill of skimming by providing them with a limited number of items, maybe three, to find in the textual material before they read. Give them these terms or occurrences and provide them a limited number of time (like two minutes) to find them. When they have found them, ask them to write down what the item means and why it is important. (Note: The same textual material can be used three or four different times with different clues.)

22. Assign different students the job of "reading tour guide." Using different sections of text, assign one piece of text to a particular student. The student's job is to become familiar enough with the textual material that he or she can then act like a tour guide through that material, saying things like, "Here on the left, I want you to notice.... (Note: This activity might take some time to get through and teachers might need to give their individual students enough time and help in playing the part well.)

23. As students are reading, ask them to copy down the key concepts or ideas from the text in single words. When they are finished, have them design a hidden word game using these key concepts or ideas.

24. Like #23, after students have read the material, ask them to construct a short crossword puzzle from the key ideas in the reading.

25. With some classes a devil's advocate approach would work well. After students have read the material, begin by asking them to discuss the key points. But without telling the students, take a stand against all the points that they make, suggesting, for example, that some minor point is far more important than the points they suggest. The purpose of this activity would be to encourage students to stand up for the points they make and, by doing so, learn more about these points.

26. Ask students to read a piece of material in a limited time span. Ask them to summarize the material in a written summary. They can share their summaries with another student to see if they are similar. Have each student add any extra material that the other student had.

27. Before students read the material, have them write the alphabet vertically down the left side of a piece of paper. As they read, have them look for a term (it must be a noun) that begins with each letter of the alphabet. Have them write the word down on their paper.

28. Before you give an in-class or homework reading assignment to students, read the material yourself and list a number of questions (maybe 20) from the reading. Divide the class into two groups and, if they haven't already, have them read the material. When they are finished, take turns asking your questions one at a time to each group. Give five points for each correct answer. If the group misses, turn it over to the other group for double points.

29. If the reading is written in chronological form (like steps in the scientific method, actions in a novel, or the events leading to the start of World War II), go through the material beforehand and list the events in mixed-up order. Write this mixed-up chronology on the board (or on a piece of paper if it is homework). As they read, ask students to arrange the mixed-up chronologies into the correct order. (Note: The teacher can cut up slips of paper and put them into individual envelopes for students to put together.)

30. Before the students read, go through the material and write down some of the key ideas, people, dates, and vocabulary from the reading. Have students read the material. For a review split the class into two groups, asking students to play charades acting out the facts and ideas. A two-minute time limit with a point given per second works well. The team with the lowest number of points wins.

31. For homework, have each student make up a 10 to 15 point pop quiz from the material in the reading. Then the next class, draw a student's name from a hat. Let this student give the rest of the class the pop quiz she or he has made.

32. After the class completes a reading assignment, split them into two groups. Play hangman using some of the key ideas, vocabulary, or people from the reading. (Note: Important sentences can be used just as easily.)

33. Give students a reading assignment (either homework or in-class) and tell them you are going to give them a quiz. As they are reading, make up a short quiz. Give it for marks.

# HOW TO MAKE THOUGHT-PROVOKING MULTIPLE-CHOICE QUESTIONS

There are two main reasons for putting this idea in this book. First, the skills of analysis are important to any sound curriculum. Second, the skills needed to address thought-provoking multiple choice questions are skills that have a practical importance for today's students, who are increasingly subjected to standardized achievement and diploma tests. Some of the same skills necessary to do well on standardized exams are dealt with in this idea. Specifically, for a student to do well on a standardized test, it is just as important to know why an answer is right or wrong as it is to know that an answer is right or wrong.

*Hint 1:* Constructing an exam like this one is often easier than constructing a regular multiple-choice exam. It doesn't matter if there is more than one right answer. In fact, if there is only one right answer the question would be almost invalid.

*Hint 2:* Don't worry about having some answers that are entirely wrong or answers that can not be supported.

*Hint 3:* Because so much credit is given to the justification and support for an answer, the test can be quite short. It will not take the place of a comprehensive exam, but would be best used in conjunction with other exams.

## Directions to Students

Most multiple-choice questions have clear answers. If you know the point, you can answer the question. But these multiple-choice questions are different. Even if you know lots about the subject, it is not always clear that the answers to these questions are right or wrong.

Here's your challenge. Read the following multiple-choice questions. Think about the answers provided. Pick the one you think is most correct. Circle the answer. Then, in the space that follows the question, write why you think the answer you chose is most correct. (In evaluating the answers you give, consideration will be given for the reasons you give as well as the choice you have made.)

*Questions*

1.  Which of the following changes in family relationships are brought about by the VCR?
    a.  Families will become less isolated.
    b.  Families won't stay at home much.
    c.  Families will become more friendly.
    d.  Families will live in the same home longer.

2.  When writing a well-constructed paragraph, why should a writer try to limit the number of sentences in a typical paragraph?
    a.  When people in today's society look at an extremely long paragraph, they feel it will take them too much work to read it.
    b.  If you can't say what you want to say in five sentences, you should quit.
    c.  The human mind has trouble remembering more than a few points at one time.
    d.  Writing briefly helps you, as a writer, focus your thoughts and avoid rambling.

3.  Which of the following can never be provided by technology?
    a.  solutions to human problems
    b.  information about people's backgrounds
    c.  security and acceptance that come from others
    d.  the ability to entertain us and prevent boredom

4.  Which of the following is not a reason why robots will take over teachers' jobs in schools?
    a.  Robots are cheaper than hiring people.
    b.  Robots are smarter than people.
    c.  Robots are not an effective learning tool.
    d.  Robots can not help students learn about career opportunities.

5.  The growth of the movie rental industry in North America is good evidence that
    a.  the importance of the family is becoming stronger in North America.
    b.  the average North American family is richer than it has ever been.
    c.  technology is changing the way people live.
    d.  people in modern society are more isolated in their homes than ever before.

# HOW TO USE GROUP WORK IN SOCIAL STUDIES

Group work fits well into any curriculum and into any subject area. Why? Because it offers students the opportunities to be active, to participate, and to contribute to the building of knowledge. All subject areas benefit from the social activity of group work. I can't imagine not using group work. To me, without group work, school would probably become little more than students writing down notes that teachers decide are important. While teachers must take responsibility for choosing important material for their students, it's not all that should go on in class.

## Practical Reasons Why I Use Group Work

1. I don't like to be "on" (in front of the class talking) all the time.
2. I want everyone in my class to talk at least once every day.
3. I believe that kids have something to say that contributes to class.
4. I want to know where kids are (what and how much they are learning), and know where I am. By listening to your students work in groups, you can get a better feeling of where they are.

## Problems That Can Eat Us Up When We Use Group Work

Although group work is beneficial, many teachers avoid it. Why? Because there are problems that must be overcome if the group work is to function effectively. Here are some of the problems you must work to overcome.

1. We forget to see things the way students see them.
2. We leave the students without directions.
3. We forget how important timing is to lesson planning.
4. We don't involve all the members of the group.
5. We expect that kids will be able to do group work right from the beginning. (We forget that they have been conditioned not to think for themselves.) We give up too quickly. If it won't work the first time, we quit.
6. We lack vision and variety.
7. We blame everything except ourselves.

8. We are too lazy, choosing to fly by the seat of our pants rather than prepare ahead.

9. We forget that there is a next year. Materials that we work hard to perfect this year can be used next year, and the year after, and the year after....

## Suggestions for Beginning Group Work

The following ideas are easy ways to begin group work in your class. Each has a simple but specific structure and a specific organizational plan. These activities are simple to set up, but they are an effective beginning. From these, you can lead to more complex group work activities.

### Idea 1: Reading-a-Text Group Work

(Reminder: Start slow.)

*Teachers:* Pick a section of content reading that you think is important. Give these directions to students.

A. You have five minutes to individually read pages and complete this activity. After you read this section, pick out what you think are the two most important points from this reading to remember. Write these on a sheet of paper.

B. (Break students into groups of four.) In your group of four have each person read his or her two points to the other group members. As each person reads his or her points, compile a list that includes each different point. (List a point only once, but keep track of how often each point is mentioned.)

C. Of all the points listed, choose the three points that your group mentioned the most times. Each person in the group should write these three points down on a piece of paper. One member of the group writes these points on a large sheet of paper and posts it on the wall.

D. Look around at other groups' points. Add any points that you think are crucial. Keep these notes in your binder for further study.

### Idea 2: Group Games

(This idea is one that puts content in students' hands.)

1. Choose ten pieces of content that are important for the students to know. This may be new content, or may be a review of recently learned material. (Note: School is a language arts experience. Have you ever considered how much of teaching is the teaching of vocabulary?)

2. Write these pieces of content on 3x5 [or 4x6 cards if the definition is long] index cards. On one side write the term; on the other write the definition. Make enough sets of cards so that you can split your class into groups of no more than five.

3. Split your class into groups of 4 or 5 students (choose the best way). Have them physically move into the groups.

4. Give the following directions:

   A. Today you are going to learn ten new and important pieces of information.

   B. I am going to go over the terms, then give your group a set period of time to go over them. Each person in the group should have one chance to be the teacher. After you have had a chance to be the teacher, we will have a contest to see which group remembers the terms the best.

   C. As the teacher, do the following: review the terms; give students time to go over the terms with each student being the teacher (monitor as you go); call the group back together; and lead in the small contest.

   D. These terms should be part of the evaluation/test for the unit of study.

# HOW TO PLAY FRONT PAGE CHALLENGE

The purpose of this idea is to help students review characters they have studied during the course of a unit. The game will probably work better toward the end of a unit, because the students will have a better memory of the content. It could also be used as an end-of-the-year review. (Although vocabulary and events can be used, for the sake of simplicity I will write the activity around the study of a character. Remember, like all these activities, you can use your creativity to shape them to your own classroom.)

## Preparation

The teacher can either make the clues or give the students opportunity to make them. Probably the best idea is to do some of each—sometimes the teacher makes the clues and sometimes the students do so. A smart teacher will save these clues from year to year. (The assignment to review and write out character sketches about the figures they have studied would be a good homework assignment.) The teacher or individual students create cards that contain pertinent information about the key figures—events, dates, places, actions and accomplishments.

## Playing the Game

If the teacher is providing the information sheets and students do not know who they are getting, the class can be divided into two teams. Team size could be altered if the class is particularly large or small. Students, seated in their desks, try to individually or if the class is manageable, as teams, to identify the person or event they are being given clues about. A correct identification would give points to the team whose member gave the correct response. For a senior high school level class, the game could be made more challenging by giving more points for a correct answer given fewer clues.

## Example

*Correctly identify this person.*

*35 points:* Clue 1—He was born in 1818 and died in 1883.

*30 points:* Clue 2—He was a German social philosopher and political activist.

**25 points:** Clue 3—He claimed that "religion was the opium of the people."

**20 points:** Clue 4—He shared a lifelong collaboration with Frederick Engels.

**15 points:** Clue 5—He dedicated his life to overthrowing capitalism.

**10 points:** Clue 6—Late in his life, he became sort of a social prophet, advocating a hard line against bourgeois elements throughout the world.

**5 points:** Clue 7—His most famous work was *Das Kapital*.

**1 point:** Clue 8—His ideas have had a tremendous influence on Communism.

*Answer:* Karl Marx

# HOW TO TEACH STUDENTS TO DISTINGUISH BETWEEN FACT AND OPINION

## RATIONALE

One of the first critical tasks of teaching is to help students learn how to judge and evaluate what they hear. Many levels of value could be placed on a piece of information. One of the most fundamental is the decision as to whether something is a fact or an opinion. An opinion may still be reliable, but it should be subjected to a different level of scrutiny than a fact.

However, not all facts are good and not all opinions are bad. Such an understanding would be overly simplistic. The activity that follows is designed to encourage the exercise of analyzing statements to discover what is a fact and what is an opinion.

Regardless of the subject area, most curriculum guides throughout North America encourage some form of critical analysis of statements. If you are to critically evaluate what you read or hear, you must be able to tell the difference between facts and opinions. When discussing the difference with students, you might want to use the following definitions as your starting point: a fact is held to be an accurate piece of information about a topic. It can usually be identified by asking one simple question, "Can this be proved?" An opinion is a personal view and cannot be objectively tested or proved.

### Directions to Students

Read the following text that tells about the Dubin Inquiry's hearings into the use of drugs by athletes. Then read the statements that follow it. Decide whether each statement is a fact or an opinion. In the space provided before each statement, write fact if the statement is a fact or opinion if the statement expresses an opinion. Be ready to tell why you chose either fact or opinion.

### The Dubin Inquiry into Drug Use in Sport

Charles Dickens begins the novel *A Tale of Two Cities* with the line, "It was the best of times; it was the worst of times." The same line could be used about Canada and the Olympic Games of 1988. One minute Canadians were on top of the world; the next minute they were at the bottom. Ben Johnson's great victory in the 100-metre dash was followed only a few days later by the humiliating and embarrassing revelation that he had cheated. He had won the race with the help of drugs called anabolic steroids.

Stories written about Ben Johnson painted the Canadian world-class sprinter as either stupid or a cheater. Ben Johnson is not entirely to blame. Like many other athletes, Ben was a victim of North America's "win at all costs" philosophy. He was like more than 75 per cent of other Olympic athletes who said YES when asked in a research survey if they would take a drug that would ensure victory in their event even if the drug would kill them within two years.

It's one thing for farmers to fertilize the crops they grow to help increase their yields. But it's another thing to "fertilize" the human body so that it will grow in the same way. Anabolic steroids have several positive uses, like helping young children fight the effects of leukemia. But they are illegal for athletes, and for good reason. They are dangerous. Rumors existed about the extent of drug use in sports, but no one knew for sure. This prompted the Canadian federal government to call an inquiry into drug use in sports. Justice Charles Dubin was given the responsibility of finding out the extent of drug use in Canadian sports.

For weeks, witnesses from many different sports were called, sworn in, and asked questions about their knowledge of drug use. Their testimony was shocking. Many athletes and coaches believed that world-quality athletes could simply not win, no matter how good they were, without using illegal drugs. It was also revealing how easy illegal drugs were to obtain, either from pushers or through mail-order firms in Mexico or Europe. Testimony outlined the damage of drug use, both to the image of Canadian sports and to the health of those athletes who had taken the steroids.

The Dubin Inquiry reaffirmed one important point about advanced technology. Being able to do something didn't make it right. Technology, in this case new drugs, did not always improve the quality of human life.

As a result of the Dubin Inquiry, both the United States and Canada will probably create legislation that carries tough criminal penalties for the illicit use of steroids. In October 1989, US Representative Mel Levine from California introduced a bill to the US Congress that places the illegal distribution of anabolic steroids in the same class as cocaine. When Levine introduced his bill in Congress, Ben Johnson attended the meeting. "I came to tell the people of this country it's wrong to cheat," Johnson said.

## Fact or Opinion Statements:

_____1. One minute Canadians were on top of the world; the next minute they were at the bottom.

_____2. Ben Johnson's great victory in the 100-metre dash was followed only a few days later by the humiliating and embarrassing revelation that he had cheated.

_____3. In one way, Ben Johnson is not entirely to blame. Like many other athletes, Ben was a victim of North America's "win at all costs" philosophy.

_____4. Anabolic steroids have several positive uses, like helping young children fight the effects of leukemia.

_____5. Justice Charles Dubin was given the responsibility of finding out the extent of drug use in Canadian sports.

_____6. Many athletes and coaches believed that world-quality athletes could simply not win, no matter how good they were, without using illegal drugs.

_____7. The Dubin Inquiry was a necessary response by Canada's federal government to technology gone bad.

_____8. Technology, in this case new drugs, did not improve the quality of human life.

_____9. In October 1989, US Representative Mel Levine from California introduced a bill to the US Congress that placed the illegal distribution of anabolic steroids in the same class as cocaine.

_____10. When Levine introduced his bill in Congress, Ben Johnson attended the meeting. "I came to tell the people of this country it's wrong to cheat," Johnson said.

# HOW TO USE GAMES FOR REVIEW:
# THE MANAGEMENT-BY-METHOD RATIONALE

Many teachers fear the energy that students seem to show in abundance. But the truth is that good students are almost always energetic students. They express themselves actively in the classroom, and they are quick to show their boredom. Good teachers know what kids are like and structure their teaching strategies to meet the energy needs of their students. Good teaching methods can help make learning enjoyable. At worst, a well-planned variety of teaching methods should help make school bearable. Often, what separates good teaching methods from poor teaching methods are chances for students to use their energy in ways that build, rather than tear down, the classroom.

*The management-by-method rationale is based on five principles:*

1. A teacher should attempt to teach every student everything, not to separate the winners from the losers. Our job is to teach, not trick.

2. Students respond positively to success and negatively to failure. The question: how can I, as a teacher, help students succeed?

3. If there is a choice between having fun and not having fun, have fun. It's OK to enjoy teaching.

4. Having fun in class does not mean forsaking standards. It does not hurt to learn.

5. There's enough time in class to finish real work. If class time is used fully, homework can be kept to a minimum. There's more to life than school.

Teaching methods should have logical and defined energy releases. There should be planned activities that take into account students' needs to move, to express themselves, and to be active. Methods are useful for different purposes. From my experience, I know that good teaching plans involve some sitting, some moving, some talking, some writing, some listening, some expressing, some laughing, and some silence. Classroom management cannot ignore the natural and reasonable activities of young humans. The energy needs of students are absolutely inseparable from their educational needs.

The charm of games is in their simplicity. Each has its own control—the rules of the game. These games are easily adaptable. The same game format can be adapted to meet the needs of any subject area or age level. The personality of the class and the teacher can be structured into the game. Timing, penalties, and rewards can be improvised by the teacher or students to fit each situation. Most of all, these games take one of the fundamental interactions of the classroom (the question and the answer) and help make that interaction enjoyable and memorable. A caution: games center on the objective level of the classroom, there is more to school that this kind of knowing. Don't be seduced by the success of games and come to rely on them to teach everything. If you do, you'll miss important parts of the curriculum.

## Game Ideas

### The Old Flash Card Game

**Principle:** Use for reviewing locations, vocabulary terms, or factual information that is best taught through redundant activity.

**Materials:** Cardboard pieces large enough for students to see from the front of the classroom.

*Suggested procedure:*

1. Place definitions, descriptions, maps, and so on onto cardboard pieces.
2. Split the class into groups.
3. Starting with the first person in the first group, hold up a card.
4. If the material is correctly identified, give the student's group 5 points. If it is not correctly identified, go to the next group, doubling the point total. (Hint: Place your notes on the back of the flash card. You can review these notes as hints.)

### Concentration

**Principle:** Students must remember the parts and match them together. The act of matching itself answers the questions.

**Materials:** Cardboard game board with thirty or so pockets (in multiples of two) where question cards and corresponding answer cards can fit.

*Suggested Procedure:*

1. Split the class into groups.
2. The first person in the group chooses two cards (one at a time) trying to match a question with an answer.
3. If missed, the cards are placed back into the pockets from which they came.
4. Proceed from group to group until there is a match. The group that matches gets the point total of the question card and the answer card.
5. The game continues until all cards are matched.

5.   The game continues until all cards are matched.

## Knowledge (like TV's Jeopardy)

**Principle:** Questions are arranged from easier to more difficult, with point totals representing the ease or difficulty of the questions. Students may choose the difficulty level.

**Materials:** Cardboard game board with categories of questions and levels of difficulty for each category. (I use five categories—like vocabulary, history, or people—and five levels of questions—from 5, 10, 15, 20, and 25 points.)

*Suggested Procedure:*

1.   Split the class into groups.

2.   The first person in the group chooses a category and a difficulty level of a question that he or she wishes to answer.

3.   If answered correctly, the group gains the number of points that question is worth. If missed, the question card is placed back into the pocket.

4.   After each attempt, move on to the next group.

## Bingo-Histo Game

**Principle:** Answers are written at random in a 25-cell bingo-square sheet (5 squares by 5 squares). As the teacher reads the questions, students mark off the correct answer. The first student to get five across, five down, five diagonally, or four corners wins.

**Materials:** Cardboard list of answers; index cards of questions; bingo score sheets.

*Suggested Procedure:*

1.   List twenty-four answers to questions that you will ask. Have students randomly write the answers to these questions on their bingo score sheets. (They can add free space wherever they choose.)

2.   Read a question, asking students to put a check in the box that contains the correct answer.

3.   The first student to complete a bingo is the winner.

4.   Question cards can be shuffled and the game replayed a number of times. (Hint: I've found that it's best not to use cover sheets. It is hard to see the answers underneath the sheets and students always seem to leave them lying around, which annoys the janitorial staff.)

## Hangman

**Principle:** The game is useful for vocabulary terms or names that you want students to know.

# WHAT WORKS

*Suggested Procedure:*

1. Choose terms or names from your content area that you wish to review.

2. Split the class into groups.

3. Write blank lines on the board to equal the number of letters in the word. Give each blank line a point value.

*Sample:* __ __ __ __ __ __ __ __ __ __ __ __ __ __ __
             1  2  3  4  5  6  7  8  9  10  11  12  13  14  15

*(The sample word is Meech Lake Accord.)*

5. The first person in the group guesses a letter. If it is a correct guess, write the letter in the correct space or spaces, giving the correct number of points to the student's team. If there are more than one of a letter, give each letter to the student. If the student guesses a letter not in the word, write the letter underneath the word.

6. Students may either choose a letter or guess at the word, not both.

7. If a student guesses the word, he or she is awarded all the points from the blank letters.

8. The student's team receives 5 bonus points if it can define the word.

# HOW TO REVIEW VOCABULARY

Vocabulary is such a large part of teaching that it would be wrong not to make as many suggestions as possible for reviewing it. Throughout this book, you will find a number of different ideas designed to help students learn the vocabulary terms found in their units of study. Here are six more ideas for reviewing vocabulary. The common thread in these six review ideas is that each helps a teacher review vocabulary within a textbook chapter.

I have put such a large number of vocabulary ideas into this book for two reasons, First, vocabulary is extremely important. Second, there are many ways to get the same job done. I don't think that I am overstating the point when I say that teachers in all subject areas are teachers of vocabulary. They teach it every day. But to use the same activity repeatedly would bore students. These ideas suggest that variety can be helpful for both the teacher and the student.

*Hint 1:* Making a number of different vocabulary reviews and getting them in good form can take some time. If you can find a friend or two who also teach in your area, split the task. First, it saves work. Second, it is a social activity and a healthy part of teaching to encourage the social aspect. (I do like group work.)

*Hint 2:* It should go without saying that if you are going to spend a great deal of time working on vocabulary reviews like these, you would be smart to carefully save the materials you make from year to year. Practice the art of recycling teaching ideas now!

## A Note about the Ideas That Follow

Each of the vocabulary reviews that follow can be created to tie into any text that students would read as part of the class. It is easy to adapt this idea to your own text.

## Idea One: Reviewing Important Vocabulary Terms in Text

*(Type: Worksheet Puzzle Review)*

You will notice that page numbers are given in this idea. My policy is generally to include page numbers with junior high school students, but not with senior high students. Until students can conceptualize how chapters are put together, page numbers help keep them on task. The job is to review vocabulary terms here, not to send students on a frustrating treasure hunt around the chapter—especially if they have not been taught the skills of understanding how a chapter and a textbook are organized.

### Preparation:

1. Seek out key sentences within the text that contain important vocabulary terms.
2. Write a short sentence stating the key concept of that block of text.

### Sample Example

Student Directions: Each sentence given here is missing a key word or words. Complete each sentence by writing in its correct completion. You may check the indicated text page if you wish. Once you have found each term, write the circled letters in order to form an important idea from the chapter.

1. __ __ __ __ __ __ __ __ __ __ __ __ __ describes the worth of a particular way of life. (p. 7)

2. Because of changes in our economy, technology, and society, most Canadians can expect to __ __ __ __ __ __ jobs two or three times during their lives. (p. 4)

3. __ __ __ technologies change our lives—maybe for the better, maybe for the worse. (p. 11)

4. The term __ __ __ __ __ __ __ __ describes the conditions of Canada's wealth at a certain time. (p. 4)

5. An __ __ __ __ __ __ __ __ __ __ process has to do with the making of things by industry. (p. 5)

6. In this book, we are defining change as all of the shifts, __ __ __ __ __ __ __ __ __ __ __ __ __, and new ways in which we do business, which businesses we have, and how we live our lives. (p. 1)

7. __ __ __ __ __ __ __ __ __ __ __ __ __ __ __ __ __ __ __ __ is a measure of goods and services produced in a __ __ __ __ __ __ __ __. (p. 8)

8. We also ask you to consider how to __ __ __ __ __ __ these technologies at the same time as they help to __ __ __ __ __ __ you. (p. 11)

9. A __ __ __ __ __ __ shower would use sound waves to wash you clean. (p. 10)

10. Canada has changed by creating new jobs to match the __ __ __ __ __ __ __ __ economy and technology. (p. 11)

11. There are jobs available to fulfill all of the needs and __ __ __ __ __ __ our society has. (p. 4).

12. __ __ __ __ __ __ __ __ __ __ __ usage has the capacity to improve both our standard of living and our quality of life. (p. 7)

13. GDP is calculated to assess the country's _ _ _ _ _ _ _ _ performance. (p. 5)

14. _ _ _ _ _ _ _ _ _  _ _  _ _ _ _ _ _ describes the way that you or your community need to live in order to feel comfortable and happy. (p. 7).

15. _ _ _ _ _ _ _  _ _ _ _ _ was the first female Governor General of Canada. (p. 6)

16. Your parents or grandparents had a different _ _ _ _ _ _ of what the future might hold for them. (p. 2)

**KEY CONCEPT:** Using the letters circled from the words above, fill in the blanks in the following sentence and discover one of the key points for the chapter. _ _ _ _ _ _ _ _ _ _ _  _ _ _ _  _ _ _ _ _ _ _  _ _.

*Answer Key:*
1. QUALI[T]Y OF LIF[E]
2. [C][H]ANGE
3. [N]EW
4. EC[O]NOMY
5. INDUSTRIA[L]
6. M[O]DIFICATION
7. [G]ROSS NATIONAL PRODUCT
8. S[H][A]PE
9. [S]ONI[C]
10. S[H]IFTING
11. W[A][N]TS
12. TECHNOLO[G]Y
13. [E]CONOMIC
14. STANDAR[D] OF LIVING
15. JEANNE SA[U]VE
16. VI[S]ION

*KEY CONCEPT:* TECHNOLOGY HAS CHANGED US.

## Idea Two: Comprehending Scrambled Vocabulary Terms

*Preparation:*

Scramble key words in their sentence contexts.

*Sample Example*

*Student Directions:* The following statements help to define important vocabulary terms that are found in Chapter Five. In each sentence the key vocabulary term is scrambled. Unscramble the word. In the space provided before each sentence, write the correct vocabulary word.

_____ 1. **mapryir** industry has to do with the production and collection of natural resources and raw materials.

_____ 2. **yrratite** industry is the distribution of goods and other services.

_____ 3. **desayronc** industry is based on the transformation of natural resources into finished or semi-finished goods.

_____ 4. **natuarrqye** industries are those industries concerned with the processing of information.

_____ 5. Labour-intensive industries which involve much physical work usually require primarily unskilled **orblau**.

_____ 6. **delklis** labour is most often associated with special training and education.

_____ 7. Some economists trace Canada's history using the **elstpa stihse** which stresses the importance of primary products to regional and national growth.

_____ 8. Fifty percent of Alfred Sung's manufacturing is done by Canadian contractors and only twenty percent is **debjob** out to overseas production, primarily in Hong Kong.

_____ 9. Some of the most remarkable **urcueltgria** changes are in crops, not equipment.

_____ 10. **scoiobrt** is one of the ways that computers are used in manufacturing.

_____ 11. Canada's primary and secondary industries rely on the tertiary industries to sell and **sidbrituet** their goods.

*Answer Key:*
1. PRIMARY
2. TERTIARY
3. SECONDARY
4. QUATERNARY
5. LABOUR
6. SKILLED
7. STAPLE THESIS
8. JOBBED
9. AGRICULTURE
10. ROBOTICS
11. DISTRIBUTE

## Idea Three: Finding Vocabulary Terms in a Hidden Word Puzzle

*Preparation:*
1.  Find key words in sentence context.
2.  Build a hidden word puzzle with those key words.

*Sample Example*

```
P R I M A R Y I N D U S T R Y G
J R I I A W E B G D T H I M K E
F E T M H U L F G U D R A I O E
P O R E R D Y O I G I O A N A E
L R D Y R Q A E F V B B O D W E
L U Y W E T F G H J K O E U L K
L K R F W E I L O U Y T N S H G
P O A O K J E A L M V I I T J R
M D N R P I Y R R W E C O R L U
L V R E I T Y R D Y S S E I P O
P O E S I T B F E R S V A A B B
L K T T Q W V T Y O I L G L A A
Q W A S G G O R L T E R D I K L
P O U M G F A J C L I H Y Z M D
W U Q L G D K U L N V X Z A E E
K D H J N S D K J F Z E G T L L
P R U O M O D E L L I K S I K L
N V C L R E S S D R G N J O K I
L E S P E X C V B N M K J N L K
S Q W S G H U Y T R F G H J K S
C O M P U T E R A G E K J H N N
B E D E D R F T G Y H U J I K U
```

**Student Directions**: Below, are definitions of important terms from Chapter Five. In the space provided, write the term that completes each sentence definition. Then circle the word in the hidden word puzzle above.

1. _____ _____ deals with using or collecting natural resources.

2. _____ industry is involved with the distribution of goods and services.

3. _____ industries are those new industries concerned with the processing of information.

4. _____ labour is generally associated with special training and education.

5. _____ industry involves manufacturing—turning raw materials into finished goods.

6. _____ _____ is work that does not take special education. Usually anyone with the physical capabilities can do this work.

7. Canada's _____ in industry is changing. The majority of Canadians are employed in the tertiary or service industries.

8. _____ is one of the ways that computers are used in manufactur-

ing.

9. Some people suggest that, with the rapid change in microchip technology, we live in the "_____ _____."

10. Canada contains about 10% of all the _____ _____ in the world. (These two words must be found separately in the puzzle.)

11. Canada's _____ started in the mid-1800s.

*Answer Key:*
   1. PRIMARY INDUSTRY
   2. TERTIARY
   3. QUATERNARY
   4. SKILLED
   5. SECONDARY
   6. UNSKILLED LABOUR
   7. PARTICIPATION
   8. ROBOTICS
   9. COMPUTER AGE
   10. PRODUCTIVE FORESTS
   11. INDUSTRIALIZATION

## Idea Four: Single Crossword Puzzle

*Preparation:*

1. Find a long, single word for the down word.
2. Find words that overlap letters with the down word.

*Sample Example*

Student Directions: In this single-word crossword puzzle, the down word is the key to solving the puzzle. All the other words in the puzzle contain letters that are part of this word. Review Chapter Two to find the answers to this puzzle. You may look for any word you choose, but just a hint. Once you have found the down word, the rest will be easier.

*The Down Word:*

__ __ __ __ __ __ __ __ __ __ __ __   __ __ __ __ __ __ __ __

is a way of doing things that involves government and some aspect of society.

*Across Words:*

1. __ __ __ __ __ __ goods or resources are rare or hard to get.

2. The __ __ __ __ __ __ __ __ __ __ of goods is the act of creating or manufacturing something.

3. A __ __ __ __ __ __ __ __ __ __ __ __ __ __ computer is equipped with transistors.

4. A __ __ __ __ __ __ __ __ __ __ economic situation is a situation

that changes quickly from economic prosperity where there is sudden growth and wealth to a time of economic difficulty.

5. __ __ __ __ __   __ __ __ __ __ __ is a branch of technology that used very long, fine, flexible glass fibres to send images of light.

6. __ __ __ __ __ __ __ __ __ __   __ __ __ __ __ __ __ __ __ __ is a means of creating or bringing into being an object of value.

7. A __ __ __ __ __ __ is a right granted by the government to someone who has the sole right to make, use, or sell an item he or she has invented.

8. __ __ __ __ __ __ __ __ __ __   __ __ __ __ __ __ __ __ __ are able to study and "diagnose" information.

9. An __ __ __ __ __ __ is a frame holding rows of counters used for the purpose of calculating.

10. __ __ __   __ __ __ __ __ __ __ __ operate on telephone lines and send pictures from one place to another.

11. __ __ __ __ __ __ __   __ __ __ __ __ provide power in the same way that gas does, but the fuel is made of alcohol.

12. The uses for oil have __ __ __ __ __ __ __ over time.

*Answer Sheet:*
*Down Word:*

socio-political technology

*Across Words:*

1. scarce
2. production
3. transistorized
4. boom or bust
5. fibre optics
6. production technology
7. patent
8. diagnostic technology
9. abacus
10. fax machines
11. alcohol fuels
12. changed

## Idea Four Follow-up: Make Your Own Single-word Crossword Puzzle

*Directions:*

The puzzles here have been included to help you review important vocabulary terms. There are many other vocabulary words that have not been used in this puzzle for Chapter 13, but are still important. The purpose of this activity is to help you review these other terms. We want you to make your own single-word crossword puzzle.

You may already have a good idea how a single-word crossword puzzle is made, but in case you don't, you can follow these directions.

1. From the chapter, choose a word or phrase that you think is important. Set two criteria for this word or phrase. First, you must think it is something worth remembering. Second, it has to include at least eight letters. Once you have picked this term, it will serve as your skeleton word. Starting at the top of the page, write this word vertically down your sheet of paper.

2. Read through the chapter. Look for other important words that include at least one of the letters from your skeleton word. Write these words horizontally across your paper, matching the letters with the skeleton word. Double check to see that the words fit together.

3. On a piece of paper, write the sentences that contain the words that go across. Keep this as a key.

4. On your "good" sheet of paper write each sentence giving a space for each letter of the missing word. Then draw a circle around the letter space that meets with the skeleton word.

5. When you have completed each of the "across" word sentences, place the letter spaces for each across word in their proper position with the skeleton word.

6. When you have finished your puzzle, try it once yourself to make sure that there are no mistakes.

7. Trade puzzles with a friend and complete the work. By the time you are finished making your own puzzle and doing your classmate's, you will have a much better understanding of Chapter 13. If you like this activity, your teacher would probably let you repeat it with other chapters in the book. It is an excellent reviewing activity and should help you do better on the class exam.

## Idea Five: Matching (Type One)

*Preparation:*

1. Find important vocabulary words.
2. Make definitions.
3. Place a space for the vocabulary word in front of each definition.

*Sample Example*

*Student Directions:* To fully understand the importance of technology in Canada, you should be able to understand some of the important vocabulary. Read the following definitions from Chapter 4 in the text. Then match the definition with the correct term listed below by writing the term in the appropriate space.

_____ 1. This occurs when our ability to consume is greater than our ability to produce. It creates a situation where there isn't enough of something to meet demand.

_____ 2. These are legal agencies or companies through which the Government of Canada or one of the provincial governments works to provide services. For example, the Canadian Broadcasting Corporation is one.

_____ 3. This is a plan for spending money. It estimates the amount of money that will be spent for various purposes in a given time by a government, business, family, or individual.

_____ 4. This is anything bought or sold; any article of trade or commerce.

_____5. These are groups of workers joined together to protect or promote their common interests.

_____ 6. This term means the selling of government owned businesses to private companies.

_____ 7. These are areas of taxation or law that are unclear. Sometimes people or businesses can take advantage of these to avoid the intent or consequences of tax law.

_____ 8. This is the amount of money which is spent over a budget.

| | |
|---|---|
| unions | scarcity |
| commodity | deficit |
| loopholes | privatization |
| budget | crown corporations |

# Idea Six: Matching (Type Two)

*Preparation:*

1. Find important sentences.
2. Take important terms out of the sentences.

*Sample Example*

*Student Directions:* Choose the correct term from the following list of Chapter 4 vocabulary that best completes each sentence below. Write the correct term in the space provided.

| | |
|---|---|
| human resources | individual action |
| means | government control |
| private control | increases |
| cooperative action | government |
| privately | wealthy |
| progressive | production |

95

government

1. Income tax is _____ in Canada. This means that as a person's income _____, the percentage of income that can be taxed also increases.

2. Private enterprise is the production and sale of goods and services by industries under _____ _____ and ownership rather than under _____ _____ and ownership.

3. Socialism is a system based on the idea that _____ _____ is better than _____ _____. In socialism, the _____ owns and controls the _____ of _____.

4. _____ _____ are the combined economic worth of the people and their skills to a country. A country with a large, well-educated population would be _____ in human resources.

5. A mixed economy is a system in which some areas of the economy are _____ controlled and some are controlled by the _____.

# HOW TO HELP STUDENTS LEARN
# HOW TO TAKE NOTES

## RATIONALE

The purpose of this lesson is to help students learn how to take better notes and to practice the skills of note-taking. Learning how to judge important information for note-taking is a skill that students should learn in junior high school and practice throughout the remainder of their academic careers. It may be that students will have had help in learning how to take notes from readings, but that skill usually needs to be honed.

My experience is that most teachers "select" notes for students and then ask students to copy these notes into their notebooks. This is helpful for learning the material, but not always for learning the process of note-taking. Making good notes is a process skill that is important for students at all levels to develop.

This lesson plan, as designed, is meant to address individual work. However, you might decide that it would be best worked as a small group (2-3 people) plan in which small groups would discuss and decide what points are important for note-taking. This lesson plan can be adapted for use with any reading material that students have access to. I think the idea works best when used in class, but it could be given as homework.

## Lesson Plan

1. There are two purposes to this lesson plan. First, the plan asks students to take notes as the teacher reads the material (or as they read it, silently or aloud). Second, as students listen, study, and take notes, they will be reviewing and learning the content of the chapter.

2. The first task for the teacher is to separate the chapter into sections for reading and note-taking. The easiest path to follow is to use each subsection as a "chunk" of material. (If your class is advanced, you may combine some of these sections.)

3. I suggest the following procedure for helping students take notes from this chapter.
   a) Ask students to get two sheets of paper. One will be for scrap and the other will be for final notes.
   b) Read each subsection of the chapter to the students (or have them read it either silently or orally).

    c) Give students a minute to write down on their piece of scrap paper what they think is the most important point from the section that has just been read.

    d) Ask a small number of students for their idea of the most important point from the section read. (There may be a number of important points.)

    e) If there is general agreement on what points are most important, write the agreed points on the blackboard. If there is no agreement, help students judge which points mentioned are most important. (Don't hesitate to give your input, as well as explaining why you came to the conclusion you did, especially early in the unit.)

    f) Ask students to write the notes from the blackboard on their good sheets of paper that will go into their notebooks.

    g) Repeat this procedure for all subsections of Chapter 14, or until the end of the class. The remainder can be assigned for out-of-class work.

    h) When the process is completed, have students put their good paper into their notebooks under the section titled Notes.

4.    As with all the chapters, I would encourage students to copy the vocabulary words from this chapter into their notebooks under the section Vocabulary. (These terms may include those highlighted at the bottom of the page, and those you have chosen to supplement that list.)

# HOW TO HELP STUDENTS SYNTHESIZE INFORMATION BY FORMING GENERALIZATIONS

**Creating generalizations helps students in at least two ways:**

- generalizations help students develop organizational structures for their thoughts
- forming generalizations helps students develop important skills in collecting and writing information. A generalization is a broad statement that describes situations that are generally true or false. Often, in textbooks, generalizations are linked together with a number of facts about the same point.

To form a generalization, there are three steps students can follow. First, collect the information or facts about the topic. Second, look for a relationship among these facts. Third, form a general statement about the related facts that summarizes them. You can test your generalization by using two tests: does the generalization say something true about all the facts? does the generalization only consider the facts and not go beyond them? The answer to both questions must be yes if the generalization is a good one.

*Sample Example*

*Student Directions:* Read the following sets of statements taken from Chapter 17. Then, in the space below each statement, choose which generalization best addresses these facts. Explain why you chose the alternative you did and why you didn't choose the others.

## I. TECHNOLOGY AND FOOD

*Facts:*

1. Food is something that every living thing on earth needs, and every living thing on earth is part of the food chain.
2. The food chain is a complex pattern of feeding relationships between plants and animals. Any "break" in this food chain can cause the rest of the chain to be broken.
3. Nearly 60 per cent of the sole caught in Vancouver Harbor have tumors. These tumors are thought to be caused by humans dumping chemicals into the harbor.

*Possible generalizations:*

- Technology can improve the food we eat, but it can also have harmful side effects.
- If our pollution causes problems in the food chain, even somewhere below what humans eat, humans may be in trouble.
- People should not go swimming in Vancouver Harbor or eat the fish caught there.

## II. THE USES OF FORESTS

*Facts:*

1. Once an area of forest has been cut, reforestation begins, and new trees are planted.
2. Controlled burns are ways that wildlife can be protected. Controlled burning allows plants to grow that provide food for grazing animals.
3. The Natural Area Program identifies areas where special ecosystems exist and works to ensure that these areas are protected from interference.

*Possible Generalizations:*

- In Alberta, decisions about the cutting of trees are made by the Department of Forestry, Lands, and Wildlife.
- Humans should be careful when they are camping or using other natural forest lands.
- Human effort can maintain and improve our forests.

# HOW TO WRITE A REPORT USING PICTURES

I remember the reports I had my junior high students do in my first year of teaching. They were terrible. I gave students a list of topics to be researched and the specific parameters of the assignment. They listened to my instructions to "do it in their own words," went to the library, found an encyclopedia, neatly copied the first 500 words they found under the topic, drew a flag for the cover and a map for the inside, punched three holes in their papers, put it all in a cover, and handed it in for a grade, expecting me to give them good grades because they were neat. Unfortunately, they had learned nothing about the topic of their report.

The whole exercise strikes me now as a waste of paper. I suspect that not one of those students remembers anything they learned as a result of that assignment. On top of the fruitlessness of the exercise, the understanding that knowledge was something "out there," out of the students' immediate understanding was further stamped on their minds.

I first designed the idea for this plan for a grade two teacher who wanted her students to learn both how to organize their thinking and writing and to learn more about birds. We used an old bank calendar and the 12 photos of birds it contained. The task was, quite simply, to have the grade two students look carefully at the pictures, list the things they could see with their own eyes, organize these things under some very general headings, and then rewrite their notes into simple paragraphs.

The plan worked well on two counts. First, students came to depend more on their own critical insights and abilities to see. Second, the task helped them, in a very natural way, learn to organize their own writing. Since using this idea for grade two, I have adapted and used the idea in many settings, from the junior high level to my graduate students in research design courses. It has always seemed to work.

Below, you will find the lesson plan. I have constructed a fictitious plan around making students look at old textbooks to discover how technology has changed over the past twenty years, but the basic outline of the plan can be adapted to suit almost any set of photos you may want to use. As it is outlined here, the purposes of this lesson plan are to

- get away from the report that is copied straight from the encyclopedia;
- have students come to depend on their own insights for their writing;

101

- help students develop an organized and systematic way to put their writing together;
- help students learn more about a particular topic (in this case, technology) and remember what they learn;
- help students become more critical thinkers and viewers.

## Lesson Plan

*Note:* This particular lesson plan is best used at the beginning of the unit, but should be used after a definition of technology is discussed.

1. Split your class into working groups. (I suggest six groups, with two groups each looking at one-third of the book. This means that two groups will look at the same set of photos so there is less chance of missing things. For ease of splitting, I would split the entire book into three parts: e.g. Chapters 1-4, Chapters 5-8, and Chapters 9-12.)

2. Hand out the instructions to students. Remind students that they are to "brainstorm" a list of things that they see in the pictures that tell them how technology has changed in the past twenty years. Their only source of information will be what they can see in the photos.

3. Before the students begin, I would suggest that you choose one photo from the text and demonstrate some of the things students might write down when they are looking at this photo. Have the entire class contribute ideas. I would encourage you to write specific points in complete sentences. Groups may have a problem if notes are written in vague phrases that other groups cannot understand. You will have time to work with groups as they are taking notes to make sure that notes are clear.

4. Ask students, in their groups, to list all the things they see about technology when they look at the pictures in their section of the book. Their task is to see and make a list of everything they can see in the pictures, but they are not to invent things or to go beyond the pictures. Remind them that they are to note everything they can see, no matter how obvious it may seem to them.

5. Ask students to look at the pictures and list what they see on paper within their group. You should expect to help them make decisions or tell them if things they list might be specific or accurate enough. When they have finished listing everything they can see from the pictures, ask them to write all their sentences on a large sheet of newsprint and put this paper up on the wall for the entire class to see. You may want to use the blackboards for this step.

6. When the notes are visible for the whole class, ask students to look at all the lists of things they can know about technology. There are a number of things they should do:

- First, they should judge the accuracy of the lists. This step can be done quickly by having groups look at the points that the other groups have written. If there are questions, you might want to ask each group to explain how the picture does illustrate that aspect of technology.
- When the evaluation task is completed, ask students to make some simple categories that would be useful in helping to collect the facts they are using—perhaps five or six categories. These should be simple categories, but you may have to help students with some of these. Some examples might be what technology looks like, how technology is used, where technology is used, how technology has changed. The simpler the categories, the better.

7. After the class has chosen the categories, split the students into new groups that represent each category listed. Give each group a particular category and instruct them to copy all the points that have to do with their category.

8. Have the groups look at all the information they have listed from the sheets of paper on the walls. Ask them to think of other ways they can organize these points of information into even smaller groups.

9. Using numbers, have the groups put each of the points in an order that seems to make sense to them. When they have listed these points in a logical order, have them write a sentence (or copy the sentence from their paper) for each point, and a paragraph for each group of points.

10. Proofread their papers and suggest improvements. Ask them to make a final copy of this paper as their report on the topic they have been given (for example, "How Technology Has Changed").

11. Help students order the class report into sections, using the original categories that they chose. Help them work the report into a unified, completed class project.

12. At this point, they should have completed a unified, complete report about technology. Have them share their work with their parents and/or some other group. They might wish to hold a panel discussion, make a video exhibit, or desk-top publish a small book about what they know about technology from their work. Later as you work through the rest of the text, you can help them test the ideas they have written in their reports.

13. Have the students keep this assignment in the writing section of their notebook.

(Note: Students have just completed, in a very natural way, research and writing. As a lesson plan that helps them learn how to write better, you might work backwards through their process to show them how important and basic the steps they took were to good writing.)

*Sample Example*

Below is an example of directions you might use with your students. Notice how clearly the directions outline the steps in the assignment. As students complete the assignment, you can have them check off the steps they have completed.

## STUDENT DIRECTIONS

Over the years, technology has changed—sometimes dramatically. The textbook you have is out-of-date, but it is filled with interesting pictures that show the technology of the day. The purpose of this assignment is to help you use your own critical eyesight and critical reasoning to discover as much as you can about how technology has changed. Your job is to follow the directions given to your group and write a report on the topic "Technology: From the Past to the Present." (You may even want to change this title later, if you think you have found a better one.)

Unlike other reports on countries, topics, or people that you may have done in the past, this report will not ask you to go to the library to find information, take notes, and then write a report. Instead, you must depend on your own eyes and your own thoughts to discover an initial answer to the question. Your teacher will be dividing you into groups, but when you are in these groups you are on your own.

Be as careful as you can. Think about what you see. Talk to other people in your group about what they see. Whatever you see, write down. By the time you have followed your teacher's directions and finished the assignment, you will have a much better idea about technology—just from looking at pictures.

Look at each picture in the section of the book that has been assigned to you. If there are no examples of technology in the picture, go to the next one. When you find a picture with an example of technology in it, ask yourself some questions. What do you see? How is technology being used? How does this technology compare to technology that you see and use every day? Using complete sentences, try to write three things about each picture. Write your notes so that other people can read and understand them. If you can think of more than three things, write down more than three. If you can't think of three, don't worry. Just write down what you see. Another group will be looking at the same pictures you are.

Follow the directions your teacher gives you and the assignment will be easy.

# HOW TO WRITE A REPORT USING REFERENCES (ESPECIALLY FOR THE SENIOR HIGH LEVEL)

The senior high research paper is often an important assignment for social studies, science, and English classes. (About the only subject area I haven't seen a research paper in is math, and I can think of reasons to write one in math as well.) It is often used as the final evaluation of how well senior high students use the library for research, find and put together the resources they find, and pull all these resources together into one big paper—The Research Paper.

Too often, however, the assignment is given, without good direction. Teachers can assume too much. Students are left to their own designs as to how to go about finding the material they need. They may not know where to find the articles and other information they need or about how to put together the material that they find.

Without some direction, the process of writing a long research paper can become quite frustrating. Below, I have listed my set of directions for senior high students about how to work. Please note that these directions are quite personal. They represent how I research in the library. Since my first job as a writer is that of a library researcher, I believe that these directions represent a tried-and-true method for doing work and organizing it. However, you or your students may have ideas about how best to do the work. If so, as always, my encouragement is to follow your own design.

## Directions to Senior High Students Who Are Completing a Research Paper

1.  If you know, generally, what you want to write, make yourself a brief point-form outline of the points that you want to make. Then, go on to 3. If you don't know what you want to write, go to 2.

2.  If you don't know exactly what you want to say, or haven't decided how you stand on a particular topic, don't worry. This doesn't mean that you can't start working. It only means that you must work and decide at the same time. Choose the general situation, question, or topic you are interested in. Let your review help you narrow the focus of your work.

3.  The first step in a review of reading material is to see if you can find

references with abstracts. (An abstract is a short summary of the article.) If you can find abstracts, even very short ones, you can save yourself a lot of time. The reference librarian can help you find abstracts in your area of interest if they exist. If you can't find abstracts, work with references that show the titles.

*Note:* Always take the time to ask the reference librarian how you might best find information. I have yet to meet a reference librarian who didn't go out of her (or his) way to help. Every single reference librarian I've me has been more than helpful.

4.  As you are working, take the extra time to make complete bibliographical references in the style that you choose for your paper. Often teachers are not concerned with the style you use, but with the consistency of that style. Check an English Handbook to see the forms you may use. A good dictionary can also be helpful. Be consistent. It may seem that you can work more quickly by not making complete bibliographical references in the style you use, but this is not true. A little more time now will mean much less time later.

5.  Set a specific number of sources that you will review (10, 20, 50, 100). In setting the number of articles you will use, don't be lazy. On the other hand, don't choose too many. Give your best guess of how many you will need, and then (unless you find you are way off) stick to this number. Review only this number. As you read, be ready to number your notes.

6.  Read the resources you have identified and chosen from your initial look at the abstracts or indexes, writing notes as you see the need. Write your notes using a black or a blue ink pen. Some of your notes will be long, some will be very short. Do not photocopy notes from the abstract or articles, unless you are going to use a long quote.

7.  Once you have taken notes on all the resources you will use, re-read them. As you are reading, write a one-line description of each note. (You are making an index of your own notes.) This sheet will become a "themes-by-number" page that states the idea of each source and gives you an overview of your work. This is a time-saving technique that makes your notes manageable in preparing to write. (Note: It may be that one article's notes could be written into several of the themes you have created. If so, split the article—always being careful that you don't lose the complete reference to the article.)

8.  Review the themes you have created and organize them by categories into a few main themes and sub-themes. Include miscellaneous as a theme. Once you have created your themes and sub-themes, put them into a tentative order and number them.

9.  Using these themes, categorize every article (or part of an article, if there are different points made) that you have taken notes about. Use

only numbers and letters for your organizing. (At this point, throw away any review that doesn't seem to fit with the paper that you want to write. They will only clutter up your work. Good writing depends more on impact than on coverage.)

10. Step back from your work and reflect on what you have learned as a result of your quick review. Draw pictures and/or write brief notes about the really important things you have noted. Speculate about what these drawings or notes mean to your work. Write notes about your own ideas at this point. Remember the two most important questions to answer in any research paper: "So what?" and "Who cares?"

11. You have undoubtedly discovered some other very interesting articles or books in the reviews you have made. But because you have been working with a limited number of references in mind, you have not taken the time to read these new ones. Take a "vacation" from your work right now and read some of the interesting things you have come across. The length of your vacation should be based on two criteria: How much time can you spare and how much interesting material have you uncovered? Take notes on your vacation.

12. Your first task when you finish your vacation is to make a final decision about what you are going to write about and the tactic, tone, style, position, and so on you will take. You are ready. Your second task is to photocopy your notes.

13. Look back over your notes as you are photocopying them. Your vacation has cleared your mind and after your decisions in #12, you will see some of the notes with new eyes. Spend a day or two buried in the reading of your notes. Take any additional notes from your reading that help you expand the notes that you have already taken.

14. Add to your outline any new notes that seem important. Since you have probably made a number of changes, photocopy your new notes.

15. Literally, cut your notes apart by number. Make sure that both the reference and the notes are numbered the same. (If you use the notes from one article for more than one theme, be especially careful to reference these with the right number of the reference.) Cut your notes again into two piles: references and notes. Put the references into a large envelope and forget about them for awhile.

16. Using your main categories, tape the notes into an order that seems reasonable.

17. Sit down with your taped notes and write. (If you have a computer, it will help you in this step.) Write a draft of the paper just as quickly as you can. Don't worry about grammar or style. If there is a new idea that you think about as you write, put it in. It is easier to fix up

something once it is on paper (or better yet, on a computer screen) than when it isn't. Finish your writing in one burst if you can. If you run out of gas, go to the next step until it's finished or you are ready to get back to writing.

18. This is where being careful will pay off in spades. Write the bibliography immediately. Use the envelope of references in the way you used your notes. Tape them to paper in alphabetical order and write them down. Make a couple of photocopies.

19. Proofread your entire paper once, making changes as you go. Make a neat copy and give it to a critical friend. (A critical friend is a person who likes you and who will tell you the truth about your work.) Ask this person to look for things that don't make sense, things that could be said better, and things that seem missing. Trust this person's judgment.

20. After you receive the notes from your friend, attend to changes the critical friend suggests.

21. Proofread your work once more and make any final changes that need to be changed.

22. Make a final copy of your paper and photocopy it one more time for your files.

23. Hand it in to your teacher, smile, and wait to collect the best grade you have ever received.

# HOW TO MAKE A CHRONOLOGICAL PUZZLE

In my experience, two difficult concepts for students were what I have named chronology and concentricity. Many junior high students, and some senior high students as well, tend not to have a problem learning about people who are alive, but often believe that everyone who has died lived on the same street at the same time. Their view of history is ahistorical. In short, for many students, the past is lumped together in one undistinguishable mass.

At the same time, students tend to memorize populations but do not apply a logical structure to these memorizations. They may memorize the population of their school, i.e. 800. They may also know the population of the town or city in which they live, i.e. 15 000. But my experience tells me that some don't know that these population numbers represent circles within circles, and that as you expand the circles outward, the outer circle of population also includes all the people within the inner circle of population. This seems like simple logic, and it is. But many young students haven't created the structure to understand this yet.

These two concepts are both important to learn and easy to teach. Let me give you a suggestion for teaching them that both stresses the concepts and is active enough to keep students interested.

## Teaching Chronology

One idea I have used to help students review chronology is the Chronological Puzzle. It can be used with any sort of data, from the life span of people throughout history to the date of important events in a particular era. The task is no different than many of the other ideas in this book of ideas. If you can organize your teaching so that two things are going on at the same time, the two things reinforce each other and the process helps students learn both.

In this chronological puzzle, the two things going on at the same time are the events to put in order of occurrence and the solution to a simple puzzle statement. The puzzle activity is simple to construct. Close to the left-hand side of a sheet of paper write down the events you want the students to put in order. On the right hand side, on the same lines as the events, put one or two words of a simple statement you want the students to remember.

3.   Here's an example, one useful for senior high. The dates to be placed in order highlight the years of important events after World War II

through the Cold War. The key puzzle phrase represents an important fact about the world at that time.

### Events from W.W.II through the Cold War

| | |
|---|---|
| The Surrender of Germany and Japan | Europe |
| Churchill's Iron Curtain speech in Fulton, Missouri | was |
| UN establishes the state of Israel | too |
| The Berlin Blockade | weak |
| The Korean War starts | to |
| The death of Stalin: Presidency of Eisenhower | escape |
| Hungarian uprising crushed by the USSR | the |
| Sputnik | impact |
| Cuban Missile Crisis | of the |
| Six-day War Between Israel and Arab countries | Cold |
| Americans land on the moon | War. |

4. Once you have the single sheet typed out, your task is to photocopy as many copies as you want, cut each single page into strips, and place the strips from one page into an envelope. Make an envelope for each member of the class.

**Hint 1:** If you are reviewing material that has been covered extensively, you might want to create an envelope for each student. If you are doing relatively new material, you might want to work in small groups.

**Hint 2:** The puzzle idea here is relatively simple. Students can work through a text or reading putting a puzzle together and constructing the dates into the time-lined order without much difficulty.

**Hint 3:** Decide which way to go—group work or individual work—and plan accordingly. It takes about 30 minutes to construct the time line and puzzle. It takes about 15 minutes to create envelopes for group work using scissors, and an hour to create enough envelopes for each student in the class.

**Hint 4:** Keep a master sheet for your files. As hard as you try to save the envelopes from one year to another, the little strips of paper are easy to lose. Good directions to students can be helpful in preserving the activity from year to year.

**Hint 5:** Once students catch on, give them opportunities to make their own envelopes. They can trade with each other in class. They will learn the material and, at the same time, help you do some of your work.

## Teaching Concentricity

Students will find that the concept of concentricity is a simple concept for such a difficult word. The task of teaching concentricity is to define the concept and to cover it simply. Once students catch on, they usually remember quite easily. The problem that most students have is that they have never thought about it, and haven't caught onto the logic of the concept. Hence, they make mistakes.

1. I have taught the concept using a relatively simple teaching idea. I prepare a template of concentric circles that I can use for all sorts of little concentricity exercises. Using a compass, I take a sheet of paper and draw some concentric circles—a small one, a larger one just outside it, another larger one just outside it, a larger one just outside that one, and so on. About seven or eight concentric circles will do.

2. Next I design a number of simple lists. In each list, the members of that list (human or otherwise) represent one element in an increasingly larger story. For example: letter, word, sentence, paragraph, page, book, shelf, library.

3. Once I have developed two or three lists, I review the concept using population figures of the local area in which I am teaching, each time giving the correct population figures for person, class, school, city, county, province or state, country, world. Even though the purpose of the activity is the concept and not the population, it doesn't hurt students to know a fact or two about the population.

4. After reviewing the concept, I place a scrambled list (not in order from smallest to largest) on the board and ask students to write the correct word in the circle where it goes. When they are finished, and it takes only a little time, I review and explain the concentric nature of the elements.

5. Next, I provide another scrambled list for students to put on their circles. This time when they are finished, I ask a student to explain the concentric nature of the elements. I repeat this about three times.

6. As a final part of the lesson plan, I ask students to come up with their own lists in groups of two. Usually one person in two will catch on easily and can help teach the other person.

*Note:* The lists don't have to have all have the same number of elements: a list of five is no different than a list of nine for teaching the concept. Here are a couple more suggestions.

## WHAT WORKS

| *Group One* | *Group Two* |
|---|---|
| Superstar player | MLA |
| Team | Legislature |
| Crowd at the Ball Park | Government |
| People in a city | Voters |
| People in a province | Citizens |
| People in the country | Residents of a country |
| People in the world | |

*Hint 1:* You don't have to provide a sheet of circles for your students. It is cheaper and takes only a little time to have them create their own sheet of circles.

*Hint 2:* You don't have to supply the whole list every time. You can start with single words, sometimes at the big end and sometimes at the small end. For example, molecule or universe might belong to the same set. Students may write different answers and still understand the concept.

# HOW TO HELP STUDENTS STUDY FOR TESTS, OR SEVEN DAYS TO A SMARTER YOU

As teachers, we usually pride ourselves on the fact that we take little for granted—that we think of, and prepare for all the possibilities. But sometimes we miss things. One of the areas most frequently missed is helping students study for exams.

Oh, we tell students to study. In fact, we remind them often that they should do it. We even give lots of not-so-subtle hints along the way that "you might want to take this down, it 'might' be on the test." Then, when test results seem to suggest that students didn't study very well, we admonish them for their behavior.

But in all my years watching teachers teach, I have yet to see a teacher actually address a process for studying for a specific exam. There are some very helpful study-skill processes like SQ3R that contain basic and generic truths about how one might study better; but even if students knew the procedures well, it might not help them on your test.

My experience suggests that we expect students to study for exams, but we don't help them very much. Does it go without saying that encouraging studying also encourages learning? Or does it seem that I am repeating myself too much when I state that the act of studying will help ensure success, which will help spur motivation, which will help ensure greater success, and will help set a cycle of success going?

The purpose of this idea is to show that teachers can help their students do better on specific, upcoming exams. At the same time, the students will be following a step-by-step process that will encourage their own learning. The format of the idea is a checklist, with a different, time-controlled tactic for each day. Within this time-controlled process is the skeleton for a study scheme that will help students do well on the exams you give them.

*Note:* Some of the skills in this format are generic; others are specific to my own exams. Read the steps and substitute anything that might be specific to your own exam ideas.

## A Study Checklist for Students Who Want to Ace the Test

*Directions*: Below you will find a daily, step-by-step system that will allow you (if you finish it) to ace the test that is coming next Friday. All you have to do is to follow the steps, one-by-one, and check each of them off as you complete it. If you complete each of these steps, you WILL get a good grade on this next test. When you have completed each day's activities, check off the activity.

_____ *Day One:* Review all the quizzes and worksheets we have done as part of this unit. Make sure that you know the answers to all the questions.

_____ *Day Two:* 1. Make a new vocabulary list of all the terms we have used in this unit. Write definitions for each term on the list. You may use the definitions in your notes. Check with me if you don't think a definition is complete enough.

2. Make flash cards on 3 x 5 index cards (or little sheets of paper) of each term on this vocabulary list. Practice these until you know them.

_____ *Day Three:* 1. Dates and Events: Find every date or event that was important in the unit (don't be trivial). On a sheet of notebook paper, write the date or event and a short, one-sentence line about what happened and a one-sentence note about why it was important.

2. Find every person who was important in the unit (don't be trivial). On a sheet of notebook paper, write the person's name and a short, one-sentence line about what that person did and a one-sentence note about why that person is important. You can ask me to do a quick check to see if your notes are complete, but not until you have at least 20 vocabulary terms and 20 dates, events, or people on your list.

_____ *Day Four:* 1. Review all your notes from the first three days. As you do, highlight the important points with a highlighter.

2. Review the unit by writing each point that you highlight in your own short-hand point form.

_____ *Day Five:* 1. Think about the content that we have just finished covering. Remember all the topics that your teacher bored you with by stating them over and over again. For example, didn't you get tired of hearing about the steps in conducting scientific experiments? Write down the five things that your teacher seemed to stress the most. It is likely that these things will find their way onto the test in essay-question form. After you have written these points down, try to remember what your teacher said. Jot down some notes.

2. I know that this is scary, but I want you to think like a teacher. If you were a teacher, what five questions would you ask about the topics you just listed? Write a question for each of the five topics.

_____ *Day Six:* 1. Look back at all your notes. Read them again. Anything you know inside-out, forget about for now. Anything you can't remember, write down one more time.

2. Look back at the possible essay questions you wrote down on Day Five. Using the notes you have, write a point-form answer for the question.

_____ ***Day Seven:*** Find a classmate who will work with you and who has done the steps outlined here. Test each other for one hour.

# *HOW TO MAKE A WORKSHEET*

Every student I know has had worksheets coming out of his or her ears. The bad news is that worksheets are often thrown together without thought in a cheap attempt to keep students busy. Most students learn to dread them. The good news is that worksheets can, and I think should be used profitably in teaching. If they are done well and used for specific purposes, they can help students learn and remember material.

## The Purpose of Worksheets

There are six basic uses for worksheets:
- as a way of reviewing important textual material
- as a way of highlighting especially important parts of a text
- as a quiet teaching method, when a quiet method is needed
- as a homework assignment
- as an assignment to grade when you want everyone to score well
- as a product that students can use to study for coming evaluations

## The Forms of Worksheets

I suppose that there are many correct forms for worksheets, but I prefer a form that highlights concrete examples from the text, complete sentences specific enough to be recognized and pulled from the text. My purpose is to make the worksheet both important and easy (quick) to complete. It is also to get students to write out the important points, vocabulary, and people's names as they complete the worksheet. It's one thing to read, but the mental activity of writing something out helps students remember it.

## Two possible examples from a senior high worksheet

*Directions:* Read the following sentences, taken verbatim from your text. Then, if you have to, look them up in your text. When you have found the missing word or name, write it both in the sentence and in the space before the sentence.

_____ 1. _____, a German professor of meta-physics, accepted the failure of speculative reason to establish the

116

truth of theology. These truths belonged to pure reason, but not to practical reason. In 1791, he published *The Critique of Pure Reason* and offered a way out of skepticism and a new foundation for scientific activity. (p. 212)

_____ 2. The revival of the constructive energy of science and all other activities after 1791 marked the beginning of the _____ and the nineteenth century. (p. 212)

*Answer Key*

1.  Immanuel Kant
2.  Romanticism

*Notice five points:*

1.  There is ample context for each sentence.
2.  Page 212 is repeated, because I think it is an important page to review. (I would skip what I thought were unimportant pages.)
3.  Students are asked to write the key term/person twice. (A simple way to help remember.)
4.  The sentences are taken verbatim from the text. (It makes them easier to find. Plus, it makes them easier to use later as a review.)
5.  Page numbers are used. (At the junior high level, I almost always used page numbers because they help students find the material faster. At the senior high level, it depends. Either way is acceptable. Presumably, students should know how to conceptualize the task of hunting for an answer.)

## A Note about Grading Worksheets

I always grade worksheets. First, I always grade things myself. Or, if it's an objective test, I might find someone to act as a grader. (But if I do, I always look at the tests later to see how students answered the questions.) It's not that I like to grade papers, but unless I have a very good reason, I don't think it's the student's job to grade other students' papers. I have found so many mistakes and so many potential conflicts when students grade papers, I just don't do it.

Second, I grade even small quizzes and assignments. They may not be worth much, but if I ask students to do them I want students to do them well. If I make an assignment, I want students to know it's worth taking seriously enough to grade.

In the worksheets I create, it would be almost impossible for a student who worked hard to make an error. Everyone should get 100%. Remember, my idea is to build from success. I want to start a cycle of success in my classes and I want students to begin the little habits of success—things like caring to do things, double checking, and so on.

# HOW TO USE HOCKEY CARDS TO TEACH ACADEMIC SKILLS

## RATIONALE

How do you encourage students who aren't interested in your subject area to become more interested? My answer: any way you can, as long as it's ethical. In my experience, junior high boys are especially difficult to motivate. Generally speaking, they may be the least interested group of students.

Still, I was a junior high school boy once a long time ago. And when I watch what they do, I notice that boys tend to like the same things I did when I was a kid. I was a baseball card collector. They, too, are often big sports cards fans. Young Canadian people, even when they don't like school much, do like collecting and trading hockey cards. This activity is based on the following principle: if the students won't come to the teacher, the teacher will go to the students.

But collecting sports cards is not limited to junior high boys. Young people of both sexes and all ages (including some people older than I) are collectors. In Canada, hockey is almost intrinsically linked to the Canadian spirit. We love our hockey. This love of hockey can easily be used to help you teach your subject area.

Below, you will find some of the activities that a teacher could use to teach skills and content in a variety of subject areas, using hockey cards.

*Note #1:* O Pee Chee is a Canadian company based in London, Ontario. It has made hockey cards for many years, and until recently held most of the hockey card market. Now they are being rivaled by glossier, more expensive cards. I have chosen O Pee Chee cards for this list of activities for four reasons: they are Canadian cards, they have the greatest amount of information and statistics on the backs, they are one of the cheapest cards to buy, and they have a large set of cards (they have a large number of cards of different players).

*Note #2:* With a little creative thought, elementary teachers can create a number of activities using hockey cards. Some of the specific skills elementary students need to learn are ordering (both numerical and alphabetical), separating by class (like teams and positions), and even artistic activities (like team colors and symbols). Although the activities that follow are more keyed to the secondary level, the use of hockey cards could be fruitful at the elementary level.

## Forty Activities Using O Pee Chee Hockey Cards

1.  Study the backs of the cards. Find the average number of different teams each player has played for. Which active player has played for the greatest number of teams? Speculate on how the player's moving might affect his quality of life. If he has a family, what difficulties might they face?

2.  Do a background study for each National Hockey League city. Where is it located? What is its latitude and longitude? What is it best known for? What are its major industries? What is its climate like? What is its history? Its population? In what ways would it be different to live there than where you live?

3.  Where do hockey players come from? Using a map of the world (and a bigger map of Canada) locate the birthplaces (countries) of all the hockey players. Once you have found where they were born, prepare a brief report that lists the countries and how many players come from these countries. Write a tentative hypothesis about why hockey players come from where they do.

4.  Using an atlas, find your favorite player's hometown. Using any resources (from encyclopedias to the Canadian Motor Association's triptik books) try to find information about this city or town?

5.  Find the hometown of each player on your favorite team. On a map of the world (and a bigger map of North America), locate each of these hometowns. Write a statement that expresses a general truth (a generalization) about the players on your favorite team.

6.  Look up the nationalities (the nation of their birth) of hockey players by position (center, goalie, and so on). Compare the number of Canadians to other nationalities in each position. Make a list (by position) of all the countries of the world where hockey players come from. Create a chart that relates position played to nationality. What generalizations can you draw from your chart?

7.  Using only Canadian hockey players and a map of Canada, place a check mark for each Canadian player in the province where he comes from. Create a chart with this information, listing the provinces in order from those with the greatest number of hockey players to those with the least number of hockey players. Find the population of each of the provinces, listing them in order from largest to smallest population. How does the number of hockey players compare with each province's population?

8.  Write down the teams from each conference. Locate all the professional NHL teams on a map. Use a different color for each conference. Speculate as to why the conferences are organized as they are. Are there any differences in travel for teams in different conferences? If so, what are they? What do you think? Could travel be a factor in a team's overall record?

9. Split up the cities where there are professional teams evenly among the class. Have each group become the Chamber of Commerce for that city. Study the cities. Prepare a brochure that highlights the attractions of that city. (Hint: the Chamber of Commerce for each city will probably send you free information if you write to them.) Plan a three-day trip to the city. Other than a hockey game, where would you visit?

10. Study economic concepts using hockey cards as the focus of the discussion. Some economic concepts that might be studied include: buying and selling, supply and demand, return on investment, marginal utility, and seasonal sales.

11. Using hockey terminology, create a vocabulary of terms and definitions that are used both in hockey and in other aspects of politics or social life. Some of the terms that might be studied include right wing, left wing, power play, short-handed, stickhandled, check, offensive, and defensive. As a project, have students try to think of other terms that are used both in and outside of hockey.

12. Study each of the team names (for example, Edmonton Oilers). What do these team names have to do with the cities? Make a list of these names and the reasons why they are used. For those which are not obvious, try to find someone who knows. (You may even choose to write to the hockey team for an answer.)

13. Prepare a survey that would find out how may people know the team names and the reason why these teams are named what they are. Make a report of results for this survey.

14. Count the number of players who have gone to the NHL from university and those who have come from junior hockey. Study and speculate about the possible difference in lifestyles for those hockey players who have gone to the NHL directly from junior hockey and those who have gone through US or Canadian universities. Write a brief paper about how these different routes might affect the player's future after hockey.

15. List all the products that a hockey player or hockey club uses (from tape to blades to zamboni machines). What resources are needed to create these products? Where do these resources come from? What is the economic impact of the creation of these resources? What is the environmental impact?

16. List all the products that a hockey player or hockey club uses (from tape to blades to zamboni machines). For each of the products that a hockey player or club uses, trace the industrial process that creates it. Beside each process, write whether it is a primary, secondary, or tertiary industry.

17. What is the average age of hockey players? What is the average number of years they have played? Try to find out what happens to hockey players after their hockey careers are over.

18. Look at the pictures on hockey cards. List every product name you can find. Make a list of the products and their names. Where (in what country and city) are these products made? What are they made of? How large are the factories where they are made? What else does the company make?

19. Look at where in the hockey draft different players are picked. The NHL has released the salaries of all its hockey players. Find a copy of this list. Compare salaries in relationship to draft choice. Study the concept 'quality of life.' Write a quality-of-life story, suggesting how much different it might be for a first-round draft pick and a tenth-round draft pick.

20. If there is a card store in your area, visit it. Find out from the card store owner (or worker) which hockey cards from years past are worth the most money. Ask why they are worth the most. Relate the answers to economic concepts you are studying such as supply and demand, and scarcity. Using what you have learned, speculate as to which current cards might be worth the most money ten years from now.

21. List the team colors for each NHL team. Find out whether these team colors mean anything special for the team. Find out, generally, how colors are thought to affect a person's psychological disposition (for example, red is thought to be a "hot" color). From what you have learned, design a hockey uniform color scheme that would reflect the disposition you would want your players to have.

22. List the team logos for each NHL team. Find out whether these logos mean anything special for the team. Think of three other logos (or symbols) that would be good ones for a hockey team to use.

23. Study the concept of trading. Using hockey cards (and team needs) as an example, show how countries, like hockey teams, trade what they have an abundance of for what they need. For example, if a team has too many forwards and needs a goalie, it trades. In the same way, if a country has oil but needs foodstuffs, it trades.

24. Look at the cards. How are they made? Try to go backwards through the process of the production of these cards, from the packaging to the cutting down of trees. How many industrial processes can you list? What resources are used in their making? Where might the plants be located? Are hockey cards a big business for Canada?

25. Find out about the O Pee Chee Company. What else does O Pee Chee make? Investigate the workings of an industry like O Pee Chee. How does a company like O Pee Chee work? Run a simulated board of

director's meeting of the O Pee Chee Company. Your task is to make five business decisions that would increase sales five years from now. Discuss the product changes you might make. Write down what five business decisions you might make.

26. Give every student an unopened pack of cards. Have the students open them. Using a current price guide, calculate the worth of these cards. Create a society with upper, middle, and lower classes based on the worth of these cards. Talk about how life might differ for people in each of these classes.

27. List the current hockey players with the highest salaries. Speculate as to why hockey players make so much money. Compare these salaries to the salaries of other jobs within society. From what you find, generalize about what this means to society.

28. List the goals of a hockey team. Discuss how a hockey team cooperates to reach these goals. What values are important to hockey teams? Relate this discussion to international and national political relationships. Make sure to discuss the concepts like values, fairness, equality, goal-setting, team play, separation of power, and cooperation.

29. Study, using both pictures and statistical information, the physical characteristics of hockey players. Create a number of research hypotheses in the area of physical characteristics of hockey players. For example, are goalies, left-wingers, right-wingers, centers, and defensemen physically different? Is age a factor? What about left-handedness? Is there a relationship between size and playing for the same team? Test your hypotheses. Do they hold true?

30. Find out where current hockey players live in the off season. Is there a relationship between current or past teams? Between where they live and where they were born?

31. List the players with the most penalty minutes. List the teams with the most penalty minutes. Is there a correlation between team penalty minutes and win-lose record? Is there a difference between penalty minutes and attitudes about following the rules (laws) of society?

32. Find the ratio of teams based in the United States to teams based in Canada. Try to find the difference in salary and income tax laws between teams based in the United States and those based in Canada. How does income tax differ in the two countries? If you can, find out how the tax monies are spent differently in these two countries. What might this tell about the relative values of the different countries?

33. List all the NHL players born in the United States. What states do these players come from? What is the climate like in these states? Is there a relationship between climatic factors and the development of hockey players? If so, what is it?

34. List all the NHL players born in other countries of the world, outside of the country where they are currently playing. Introduce the terms immigration and emigration. Speculate about the cultural differences between countries and the possible difficulties of moving. Discuss whether being a hockey player makes it easier or more difficult for a person to emigrate from another country. Use this discussion to focus on historical immigrations to Canada.

35. What incentives does O Pee Chee use to encourage people to buy hockey cards? List these. Examples might be: gum in the package, completing a set, number of cards in a pack, packaging, relatively cheap price per unit, possibility of trading with others or selling at a later date. Study the concept of economic incentives. Relate O Pee Chee's attempts at other types of economic incentives used by other, unrelated companies.

36. Pick your favorite team. Note all the different places that some hockey players have moved during their careers. Draw a map that shows the Incredible Journey of _____. Do an oral report that traces a particular hockey player's history, speculating how life changed for the player as he moved. If you live in a hockey city, invite one of the players who has moved the most to talk to your class. Ask him to talk about the difficulties and good parts of moving from one city to another. If he is married, invite his wife as well.

37. Have students choose the birth years of their favorite hockey players. Research that year to find out what important events were happening in the world. For example, what national and international events occupied the minds of Wayne Gretzky's parents when Wayne was one year old?

38. When a hockey player finishes the season, he goes home. Choose a number of different hockey players who live in North America. Pretend that the player is going to drive home and take a well-deserved vacation at the same time. Using information like Canadian Motor Association trip books, plan a trip route and agenda for the hockey player that would take him to some of the sights along the way home. If that player traveled 300 km per day on a more-or-less straight route, where could the player stop? What could he see along the route?

39. What historical figures have the same first or last name as your favorite hockey player? Make a short list of these people. Look two of them up in an encyclopedia. Prepare a short oral report on these figures to give to your class.

40. Make a chart of the populations of the NHL cities. What other large North American cities do not have NHL teams? Speculate on reasons why they might not.

# HOW TO TEACH STUDENTS TO MAKE THEIR OPINION KNOWN TO THE GOVERNMENT

There is an old joke with the punch line "This is what you'll look like if you don't drink your milk." Almost everyone has been taken aside by a parent and shown the bad example. The message is always "Don't be like this!"

Sometimes teachers forget the power of using bad examples. Especially when they are humorous, they can be used to point out problems and tell students "Don't be like this!"

The purpose of this lesson plan is to help students prepare a point of view and express it to one level of government in written form. I believe three things:

- Democratic governments can only be responsible by seeking and attending to the expressions of opinions by their citizens;
- Citizens must make their views known to their governments;
- When making their views known, citizens must not let the bad form of their presentation get in the way of what they feel they need to say.

Therefore, I believe that this plan encourages students to accept their roles as responsible citizens in a democracy.

Writing to a governmental representative expressing a concern or a point of view about an issue of current importance is a responsibility that should be done with consideration and preparation. Learning the responsibility of a citizen to make personal views known is important. But citizens should know that government representatives (anyone, for that matter) have more to do than read "some half-baked letters from a bunch of school kids." If this lesson idea is to be done, it should be done well.

Depending on your class, you might want this assignment to be an individual one, a group one, or a whole class assignment. Each choice has its own advantages.

One necessary (at least very helpful) item for this lesson plan is a copy of a good Canadian dictionary, one with a comprehensive Secretaries' Guide. Within a Secretaries' Guide, students can find much important information about letter writing. The sections of "Forms of Address for Governmental Officials" will also be helpful in putting the letter in proper form. Although this care is not necessary, it is always best to do something right if you're going to do it. Plus, if students don't already know how helpful a good dictionary can be, this lesson can highlight the fact.

## Lesson Plan

1. Write these five words on the board: clearness, conciseness, completeness, courtesy, and correctness. Tell students that these are the five criteria for judging the power of a business letter. It's not just that you want the letter to look nice. If you are going to write about something you care about, you want your point of view to have punch and power. You don't want a governmental official to think you're not worth giving attention to because you don't take the time to spell her or his name correctly.

2. Review what the five terms mean. Give students Handout 1 as a helpful guide for their reference.

3. In order to help students review some of the problems, give them the letter in Handout 2. Remind them that this is an example of a poor letter, one that breaks many of the rules cited in Handout 1.

4. Ask them to read this letter with a red pen in hand. As they do, have them circle every mistake they can find in the letter.

5. Using Handout 1, help them discuss why the letter is a poor example of a letter to a public official.

6. After looking at the problems with the letter, have the students decide what issue they are going to write about. If students are working alone, they might want to think about the issue overnight. If they are working in groups, they can discuss the issue in their group and make a decision there.

7. After the issue is chosen, use Handout 1 as both an evaluation checklist and a set of directions to follow.

8. Have students finish their letters and share them with each other, as critical readers. As a teacher, check the letters for problems.

9. At this point, I encourage that you send the letters—especially if they do not violate the standards set up in Handout 1.

## Handout 1:
## Essentials for a Proper and Powerful Letter to a Governmental Official

1. Clearness: A letter is a message to a reader. If the reader can't understand the message, the letter is a failure. Clarity can be better achieved by following these simple steps:
   - Make sure you know what you want before you write your letter.
   - Write down specifically what you want to say in note form.
   - Choose and check the words you use carefully—avoid vague terms.
   - Don't write sentences that are too long.
   - Consider the reader and try to match his or her intelligence.
   - Double check your punctuation, paragraphs, and grammar.

2. Conciseness: Since governmental officials receive many letters each day, it is best to get right to the point. The best letters allow the reader to get the point quickly. In working towards conciseness, follow these simple ideas:
   - Don't leave out important facts, but don't put in facts that aren't important.
   - After you have written your letter, go back and take out repetitive comments.
   - Look for ways to turn long expressions into shorter ones.
   - Have someone else review your work for parts that could be shortened or taken out.

3. Completeness: Every point needed to explain your view should be included in your letter. The best way to gain completeness is to take notes before you start. In working towards completeness, follow these simple ideas:
   - Make a "grocery list" of items you want to mention before you start.
   - Order these in the same order you want to put them into your letter.
   - Reread your letter to see if you have everything in it.
   - Have someone else review your letter, looking for parts that should be added.

4. Courtesy: The success of a letter often depends upon persuasion. Rude and cynical comments will make the reader believe that any point in the letter is worthless. True courtesy, on the other hand, considers the problems, needs, and feelings of the reader—even though the reader may be a public official. Written words are etched in eternity. A rude or quickly chosen written word, done in the heat of the moment, can come back to bite the writer. Written words have a permanence that oral language does not. In working towards courtesy, follow these simple ideas:
   - Choose the proper salutation or closing to your letter.

- Show respect for the character and dignity of the reader.
- Do not use sarcasm, abuse, or name-calling.
- Do not over-exaggerate expressions or thanks or problems.

5. Correctness: Letters should not contain errors. In other words, before you write a letter, do your homework. Correctness also means correct form. Even the best written letter suffers if there is no attention to correct punctuation, spelling, or grammar. In fact, problems in these areas give a bad first impression and can label the letter writer as unintelligent. This label eliminates the power of the letter. In working towards correctness, follow these simple ideas:

- After your letter is written, but before its final form, check for errors in these areas: grammar, spelling (including people's names), capitalization, punctuation, abbreviations, and factual information.
- Have a friend review the letter for you, just to make sure.
- Make a final copy with care, double checking before you finish.
- Follow rules for spacing and form.

## Handout 2:
## Letter to Mayor Roberts

Joe Roberts
mayor
Edmontun, Altba

Dear Joe——

Your a geek! My father says so and I knew it now. You ain't never done nothin right since you took office and I guess you never will. Thies is yor're latest mistake. On July 34, 1993, the RCMP raided a party we were having in our neighbor's field and made us all leave. We was having a good time and we wasn't hurting nothin. The fire wasn't our falt at all.

We think that police should leave peaceful citizens alone unless they are doing things that really hurts others. There were four things that they did that were wrong.

We pay taxes and we think that our taxes are better spent than having police harass citizens who pay taxes to police so they can protect citizens who pay taxes, if you know what I mean!!! So next time don't do it.

In closing, we think you are probably a good guy that just doesn't know whats going on. This is why we wrote this letter. Now that you know, please, please please plasse do something about it.

Thank you for your help.

Sincerely,

Your taxpayer citizen